HERITAGE BUILDERS

THE LEGEND OF
GEORGE JONES

....

CHARLENE MONTGOMERY

with Earl Peanutt Montgomery

HERITAGE BUILDERS PUBLISHING
MONTEREY, CLOVIS CALIFORNIA

HERITAGE BUILDERS PUBLISHING
©2014 by Charlene Montgomery

First Edition 2014

Contributing Editor, Dr. Sherman Smith
Cover Design, Carolyn LaPorte
Book Design, Keith Bennett
Published by Heritage Builders Publishing
Clovis, Monterey California 93619
www.HeritageBuilders.com   1-888-898-9563

ISBN 978-1940242-20-0

Printed and bound in the United States of America.

HERITAGE BUILDERS

Cover Photo Photography: Michael Ochs Archives
Collection: Michael Ochs Archives
Tammy Wynette photos courtesy of BMI Archives

....

Dedicated to
Victoria Rae Bullion
(my granddaughter)

TABLE OF CONTENTS

Contents

ACKNOWLEDGMENTS

Charlene Montgomery

I wish to thank my husband, Earl Peanutt Montgomery, for his understanding and encouragement. Without him, this book could not have been written.

I wish to thank Dr. Sherman Smith for believing in the book and for his willingness to publish it. He spent countless hours writing, editing, and working to make the book a reality.

I wish to thank my agent, Paul Chisenhall. He introduced my publisher to me and spent his time helping bring the book to a contract. I thank his wife, Beth, and his two daughters, Lauren and Lindsey. They spent many hours typing from handwritten transcripts that made the editing possible.

I wish to thank Steve Turner and his wife, Sherry, for the time they spent making sure the correct information always got to our Publisher and for all the encouragement they gave to us.

SPECIAL FRIENDS

Dallas and Sharon Frazier made an impact on my life, and their influence has made me a better person. I cherish their friendship.

Jimmy and Sue Richards have been loyal friends for over fifty years. We share together so many memories of George Jones and Tammy Wynette.

Billy Robertson remained a true and loyal friend through all the good and bad times Peanutt and I experienced through the years.

Jimmie, Frances, and Meloni Raburn for their love and support through all the years that we've been friends.

Gail and Sheila Murray for the love, respect, and friendship they have always shown.

Gary and MaLea Scales for their friendship, love, laughter, and for the many fun times we've shared.

April Kimbrell is a special friend to Peanutt and me.

Gay (Willingham) Cole for being my friend since my childhood. She is as close as a sister to me.

Connie Spencer is my aunt, but she is more like my sister. She's always supported and been there for me.

Nital Patel is a special person in my life. She will always be a part of my family and me.

Johnny Kindred is my long-time George Jones loving buddy.

Mark Holt is my nephew and has a special love and care for us.

Charlotte Carmack is a good friend and is so bubbly and full of joy.

Brother Tom and Verna Malone is our Pastor and wife. They spent a lot of time with George, Peanutt, and me encouraging us to live better lives and to become better people.

Bill Allen of Spurger, Texas is a dear friend and first cousin of George Jones. Bill called many times wanting to know if this book is finished, and it finally is.

SPECIAL THANKS TO MY FAMILY

Irene (Green) Bentley was such a loving and caring mother. I have never known a greater love than my mother had for me.

James, Travis, Harold, Kenneth, and Jerry Green are the best brothers I could ever have.

Nell Lee, Paulene Thomas, and Linda Welborn Jones Dodson are extra special to me because of the closeness we've shared as sisters.

Teresa True Hartzog Bullion and Dorothy Montgomery are my loving daughters. They have proved that broken fences can be mended, and the chain of love has no weak links. Their loving bond will hold us together forever.

IN LOVING MEMORY

James Alvin Green was my caring but stern daddy. He faithfully provided for his wife and nine children. The very threat of his belt kept me out of a heap of trouble. He died of heart failure at age fifty-four.

Don and Patricia Gentry lost their lives on April 27, 2011 when a tornado hit Phil Campbell, Alabama. I was talking to Patricia on the phone when she and Don were blown away. They were special friends, and I miss them.

Kevin Whorton was our DJ friend who played our music for twenty-four years on WLAY Radio in North Alabama. He was a dyed-in-the-wool George Jones fan.

Bobby LaFaye Taylor of Panama, Oklahoma lost his life to a heart attack. He was a dear friend, and a major help in our church and ministry.

Jimmy Russell of Pearland, Texas. Jimmy was a dear friend and George Jones' first manager. Jimmy's mother was so proud of him being on the road with George because she trusted Jimmy so much.

All the Praises and anything good that should come out of this book are to be given to our Savior The Lord Jesus Christ.

Tanya Tucker

I have known Charlene and Peanutt Montgomery since I was a little girl. My daddy and mother brought me to Nashville when I was nine years old seeking to record my first song and to help my family with the expenses of staying in Nashville, the Montgomery's asked us to come and stay with them for a while. I love Charlene and Peanutt and have known and been friends with them all my life. Charlene and I wrote a commercial for Sealy Mattress Company one time, and I have recorded some of Peanutt's greatest songs. My first number one hit was *"What's Your Mama's Name"* one of Peanutt's greatest songs in my opinion.

I believe of all the people who knew and loved George Jones, Charlene Montgomery is among the most qualified to write this book. She knows the life of George Jones like no other person. She was with him through the heartaches, troubles, battles that raged through him, and yet she defended George and loved him for whom he was. Charlene was with him during his marriages, the birth of his children, and the storied career as George and her husband Peanutt became one of the most famous teams of singer/songwriters in music history.

I was asked to write this Foreword by the Publisher because of my life-long friendship with George, and I count it a privilege to do it. George was my loyal friend, my mentor, and I could call on him for anything I needed. He would always have time to talk to me about serious matters, or we would just enjoy each other's company and have fun singing, making up songs, and being ourselves. We were known to pull some stuff on occasion and get ourselves in a bit of trouble.

I know the circumstances that played a role in some of George's behavior, but people judged him who didn't really know him. He was a good man with a kind heart, and he certainly took an interest in me and helped my career. I had the privilege of singing at his funeral; a moment in time I will cherish forever.

You will love this book because Charlene, in her colorful vernacular, tells it like it is and takes no prisoners. She took nothing from George Jones she didn't want to take, but he respected her and loved her from the moment he met her. He was her friend. In this book, Charlene sets the record straight and shows the other side of George Jones you won't read in the tabloids and hateful books written by people who were jealous of his accomplishments. He was and will remain The King of Country Music.

Tanya Tucker
Multiple Grammy Award Winner

How This Book Came to Be

It has been my privilege to work with Charlene Montgomery on this book. I am the first to admit that I had no country music background and didn't know much about George Jones or his life. I followed the stories of George and Tammy Wynette and was sad when their marriage came to an end, but I had no clue why or how that happened. Today, I am a huge fan of George Jones and Country Music. I know this man, his family, and his story.

I received a call from Paul Chisenhall, Agent for Charlene Montgomery, and he asked if I would be interested in talking about an author he was going to represent. I agreed, and I made the trip from California to Muscle Shoals, Alabama where the Montgomery's live.

I had heard of Muscle Shoals and knew that some major stars had come out of there but had not been in the area before. I was struck that this small place had such a pedigree of big singers and music producers. Paul presented me with a manuscript entitled *The Good Side of George Jones.*

The Montgomery's, Paul Chisenhall, and Steve Turner, who is an independent music producer, and I met at Shoney's Restaurant in Sheffield, Alabama. We literally went through two meals, and I was introduced to Peanutt's song writing ability by the music that was playing in the dining area. Almost every five minutes, they were playing a song that Peanutt had written or co-written, and I was introduced to a couple of talented music geniuses that I had previously never known.

I was awarded the contract to publish the book, and it was then that I asked Peanutt if he could write a song with the same title as the book. We changed the name to *The Legend of George Jones,* and Peanutt had the song, *The Legend of George Jones,* written by mid-afternoon. That song, along with several other songs written by Peanutt Montgomery and sung by George Jones, is included on a CD as part of this book. This concept of a legend singer with his main legend songwriter of thirty years merging into an album and book with the same title has never been done before and is not likely to be done again. You are reading a piece of music history.

Charlene Montgomery is a colorful and pleasant lady who is extremely talented. It has been a pleasure working with her. She did an excellent job keeping the timelines, dates, names, and information as accurate as I have ever seen done over such a long span of time. Charlene truly is the only person qualified to write this book. She was with George Jones through five marriages and the birth of all his children. She knows George Jones better than most of his wives do. She and Peanutt were with George most of the time for years, and Tammy Wynette was Charlene's best friend.

I got involved with George Jones and his family through this book. Sue Jones, Jeffery Jones' wife, was instrumental in keeping me informed about the events that took place from the Jones childrens' point of view through the years with their famous dad. Story after story unfolded, and it would take a library to contain all the books that could be written about this legendary singer.

I know you will enjoy the book and the music.

Dr. Sherman Smith

THE LEGEND OF
GEORGE JONES

....

CHAPTER ONE

Memories of the Big Thicket

The look on George's face clearly shows that he enjoys talking about his childhood days. He lived in a small community in East Texas, known as "The Big Thicket." His memory in the last days of his life was as keen as it ever was and allowed him to spit out stories of those days as vivid as if they had only happened yesterday.

Most people that lived in The Big Thicket were considered to be poor people. George referred to them as just good ole country people, "Souls that worked hard for hardly a living," he would say. Those days were tough for George and his family. Everybody felt the licks of The Great Depression. Each family lived and accepted their own way of life and few, if any, knew any other way of life even existed. The Jones family was no less fortunate than the majority of the rest of the folks that lived in The Big Thicket.

George Washington Jones, George's father, was a hard worker. He was a logger as well as held other jobs from time to time. He was a heavy drinker, but he provided well for his family. They always had a big garden and plenty of food on the table. Clara (Patterson) Jones, George's mother, was a Christian lady. She was a very kindhearted and humble person who treated everybody the same. She loved people and was very much a loving mother to her eight children. Mr. and Mrs. Jones had two boys and six girls and were a close-knit family. The boys' names were Herman and George Glenn. The girls' names were Ethel, Helen, Lois and Joyce (twins), Ruth and Doris (also twins). Ethel died at the early age of 8 years old from Malaria fever. She was the apple of Mr. Jones' eye, and he loved her so very much. Ethel's death is blamed for Mr. Jones' heavy drinking because he couldn't handle losing his little girl. He'd drink to help wash away the pain, but it never weakened or even faded his love or memory of Ethel. Helen spoke highly of her dad, and she talked about how hard he worked to provide a living for his family. She recalled his love for music. She said he didn't go to church, but he'd always go to the old "brush arbors". Sitting under the open-sided shelter he loved to listen to the gospel music and singings.

Most of the people that lived in The Big Thicket were good people. They produced a way of life that was somewhat different from the folks that didn't live there. They maintained their own set of rules, morals, and values to live by. Their standards were important to them, and most all Big Thicket families honored these community values. George held to those principles and never let go.

On September 12, 1931, Clara Jones gave birth to a twelve-pound baby boy and named him George Glenn Jones. She adored that baby, and she became as fond of little George as Mr. Jones had become of Ethel. Mr. and Mrs. Jones were experiencing marital problems when George Glenn was born caused by the heavy drinking of Mr. Jones. Mrs. Jones simply turned her attention to the newborn child, and her interest in the baby became her primary focus. Mr. Jones had begun to get a little more rowdy when he was drinking, and Mrs. Jones was getting a little more fed up with him. Clara gave all she could give to Mr. Jones, but George Glenn began stealing her heart. George was about six years old when he and his siblings were all beginning to sing around the house, especially George and Doris. Although all the kids were musically talented, it was George who loved music the most and began as a young child to demonstrate his talents.

I could sit for hours and listen to the stories George would tell about his life back in those days.

He'd say things like, "I can still smell that scent of mama

cooking breakfast, country ham, red eye gravy, eggs, and biscuits. There's just nothing that smells that good today."

I recall him saying, "I miss the sound of the wind whistling through those tall pines."

These were hard times, but there were also good times.

"You know those people back then were happy people," he'd say, "they lived hard, but they accepted it. It wasn't a big deal to them; they got by just like everybody else."

It was obvious that George held a special place in his heart for those people from his childhood. If time could roll life back to the old days, he probably wouldn't want to live that kind of life again, but money couldn't buy those precious memories of when he had a living mom and dad, five sisters, and a brother. They're all gone now except one sister, Helen. Those days are a part of him that molded him into the man he became.

George finally got his first guitar and started learning how to play it. With the help of a little old lady that went to church with him, he learned to play it in a very short time. Her name was Annie Stephens, and she was the wife of Brother Burl Stephens, who was the pastor of a church that George had been going to in Kountze, Texas. The Jones family had been attending this little non-denom-inational church for quite a while, and George would get up and sing at the services. Bro. Burl and Annie held revivals and gospel meetings all over Beaumont on Saturdays, and George would go with them and sing to the crowds. People thought he was the most amazing little fellow they'd ever seen. People loved him and told others about him, and folks would come from all over the county to hear him sing. He was young and shy, but the shyness seemed to melt away little by little as he began to realize that people really liked his singing. There was nothing George liked any more than playing and singing, and the larger the crowds he drew the happier he became.

George wasn't too fond of having to sing for his daddy in the late hours of the night. Recalling his childhood days, George said his dad would come jolting in the house, wake him up, and demand that he sing to him. He would always obey his dad's command, but it wasn't because he wanted to; it was because he was afraid of him, and Mr. Jones could get plenty rough when he was drinking. If there was ever an instance when George hated to sing, this was the time. If there is a good side to Mr. Jones, it would have to be that he knew his children had talent and wanted them to put it to good use even if it wasn't for anyone but himself. Mr. Jones enjoyed his kids' singing because he loved music. He loved the old Roy Acuff, Bill Monroe, and Hank Williams, Sr. tunes he'd listen to on the radio.

I always enjoyed the stories George would tell about his childhood and his family. Sometimes, he'd pick up his guitar and sing his mother's favorite gospel song, *"Nothing Between My Soul and My Savior,"* and tears would run down his face. George had a wonderful family, and I had the pleasure of meeting every one of them (except Ethel, of course). Ruth was quite a character, and she talked all the time. She really wanted to look out for George, and she came and visited George more than any other sibling. She was jolly and a lot of fun to be around. She was born in March and very much believed in her "Aries" sign. She was a real estate agent, and George used to say she'd talk her way out of more deals than she'd ever close. Lois was a real sweet and humble lady. She didn't want to get involved with George's business at all but was always very concerned about her brother. Doris came to visit with George often but not as much as Ruth. Doris was quieter but wasn't afraid to speak up when she felt it necessary to do so. She was also concerned about George and his happiness.

Joyce was the last sister I met, and it was later on in life that I got to know her. Peanutt and I were in Vidor, Texas singing at a church, and Ruth came to see us. She told us that Joyce was in a nursing home, and we wanted to go see her. The next day we went to visit her, and I took a quilt that I had made to give to her. It had Bible verses on it, and she couldn't believe that I wanted her to have that little quilt. She was so thankful we came to see her and was so proud of that little quilt. She was a very sick little lady, but she felt pretty good that day. She knew who we were and asked us about her brother George. We told her that we seldom ever saw George anymore but from what we heard, he was doing really well. We had a very good visit with Joyce and had prayer with her before we left. I was really glad we had gone to see her because it wasn't long afterward that we heard she had passed away.

Helen was the sister that George always talked about. He loved all his sisters and his brother, but she was the one he seemed to turn to when he needed advice. Helen was a real reasonable person. She was serious minded and was blessed with plenty of intelligence. Helen could be counted on to do the right thing in every situation, and I think she was a mother figure to George. Helen and George were close because she was the oldest sister, and he was the baby. George really thought a lot of Helen's husband also, and he'd tell me stories of how Mr. Scroggins would buddy up to him and get him to help in the fields to kill out the grasshoppers. All these experiences made George very fond of Helen and her husband.

I was only around Herman a few times, but I recall this one visit in particular. We were in Vidor, Texas with George, and we went by to see Herman and his wife, Evalene. They were such sweet down to earth folks, and Herman was very much a family man. Living with him was his precious little autistic grandchild.

It was obvious that Herman loved his little brother George, and my heart was really touched as we started to leave. George noticed that Herman had a flat tire on his car. George reached in his pocket and took out some large bills and laid them in Herman's hand. Herman thanked George over and over and told George that he didn't need to give him the money, but George just smiled at him and walked away.

When all the siblings had passed away except George and Helen, George's memories of them never faded. From time to time, George would share memories of his childhood days that would take him back to his roots in The Big Thicket. It was amazing how George could pour out stories of those days of his youth and paint a picture in your mind as clear as if you had been there with him. Time, fortune, and fame will never be able to erase those memories George held so dear to his heart of his family, his childhood, and the experiences of the life he lived in The Big Thicket.

Peanutt and I have traveled to The Big Thicket many times when we'd be in East Texas on tour, and we loved to go there.

We would recall and dwell on all the stories George had told us about his life growing up in that area. Even though the area has changed a lot since those days of George Jones, I still imagine it just as he described it so many times.

George talked a lot about his father and mother. He said his dad played the guitar as well as the harp, and his mother played the piano and organ. He said she played the organ for the church they attended. He also knew he was very special to his mother; she let him get away with murder, and she didn't make him do any chores like the older children had to do. He was spoiled by his mother's love, but he loved every minute of that spoiling.

When George got his first guitar, he would find somewhere he could be alone, so he could practice and learn how to play it. He'd do anything he could to find the time to pick and sing, which was his passion. That love for country music lived within him, just like the love for his family.

There was a little restaurant in Vidor, Texas, where George's mother, Clara, loved to eat. It was called, "The White House." George said he'd always have to take his mother there every time he went to visit her. He'd say, "If I go to Vidor, I'll have to take mama to The White House." Then he'd smile. It was abundantly clear that he liked that expectation from his mom.

CHAPTER TWO

The Streets of Beaumont

When George would tell the stories about how he started singing for the public on the streets of Beaumont, Texas, I would sit for hours listening and visualizing George as a boy getting thrilled from playing for the people on the streets. He'd take his guitar and play for anyone who would listen. He never played for money and never expected any. He loved to play and sing, and that's about the only reason he'd get up in the morning. School, books, and learning were far from his mind, and so was everything else except learning how to play his guitar and sing. It wasn't unusual for him to skip school and use that time for practicing.

George's simple methods of entertainment began to impact people, and they liked him a lot. He had a little tin cup he would place in front of him on the sidewalk, and people began throwing change in it. Although George didn't expect much, he was thrilled that at the end of the day, he would have collected several dollars. That was a lot of money for a poor little boy who wasn't used to having much. When he finished his performances, he'd have enough money to go to a movie, buy some ice cream, get something to eat, and still have enough left for a piece of bubble gum. Sometimes George would bring home more money than his daddy would earn from a long day of logging. George never got spoiled but always appreciated the folks showing him love by giving him a little money for his talents.

George played and sang the entire time he was growing up.

He was approached one day by a couple singing as a duo and entertaining at the Beaumont Playground. George wasted no time and joined "The Eddie and Pearl Show."

George's dad and mom were having serious marital problems. They were not getting along, and they started drifting farther and farther apart as they were going their separate ways. George began staying away from home. He would live with different relatives, and sometimes he'd stay with Eddie and Pearl.

George Glenn didn't like being at home with all the turmoil going on between his parents, so it was rough on him. George loved his dad and mom and was missing his home life, but things got worse for him because Mr. and Mrs. Jones moved back to Vidor, Texas. George remained in Beaumont because he could continue to sing and make a little money to support himself.

He continued his gigs with Eddie and Pearl at the Beaumont Playground, but he was barely making enough money to support himself. He'd pick up other work when he could find it, but he was between a rock and a hard place (as he put it). As a teenager, he was too young to play the clubs and dive bars. George wanted to play the bars because he could make a lot more money, and it was way more exciting, so he would lie about his age and get in. He got away with this many times before getting caught because he was only a young teenager struggling to make ends meet.

Many, many times I've heard George say, "I didn't sing for money and didn't even expect it; I just wanted to pick and sing for anyone who would listen."

He said over and over, "I wasn't trying to be a star. I never even thought about that. I just loved doing what I was doing. Of course as I got older, I had to have money to survive. Becoming a star never crossed my mind; it just turned out that way."

George Jones was thankful for his success as a singer, but he never expected it to lead him to what he became. He excelled far beyond the streets of Beaumont to become the King of Country Music.

CHAPTER THREE

Dorothy Bonvillian -
Wife Number One

George Jones's life was about to drastically change. While working with Eddie and Pearl at the Beaumont Playground, George met a young and beautiful dark-haired, dark-eyed daughter of a banker. Her name was Dorothy Bonvillian. Immediately, the two were attracted to each other, and the "sparks" began to fly.

George was only eighteen years old when this happened. He was lonely and desperately in search of companionship, and a key that would unlock the door to his unhappiness. He wanted a family and home, and Dorothy's parents provided this need because they were fond of George. He spent a lot of quality time with the Bonvillian family.

In 1950, Dorothy Bonvillian became the first Mrs. George Jones. George was now happy. Even though George and Dorothy lived with her parents, George felt he had finally found acceptance into a family and a permanent place to call home. George continued working for Eddie and Pearl, and his reputation around the Beaumont area as a great singer was making him very well known.

Dorothy became pregnant with their first child. George was thrown for a loop when his wife announced that she was expecting, and he began to wonder how on earth he could provide for a wife and a child? In spite of the obstacles that confronted him, he would put forth every effort to fulfill his responsibility of taking care of the young Jones family.

The Bonvillian's were better off financially than most people

George had been around, so he had to become accustomed to several attitudes that would bring about even more changes for him. Mr. Bonvillian did not believe George could ever make enough money with his music to provide a decent living for his daughter and grandchild. He felt that working only on the weekends picking and singing was too little income to rely upon. He secured a job for George painting houses. Mr. Bonvillian decided that a regular job with weekly pay was exactly what George needed to support his family.

George was not at all happy with his painting job. He was a singer, and that's all he wanted to be. Music was all George had ever done, and that's all that was on his mind. George would much rather strum a guitar than slap paint on a plank with a paintbrush. His heart was very heavy. I have often wondered what kept him from writing the lyrics to a song on one of those houses with his brush.

It wasn't long before there were some serious disagreements between George and his in-laws. After a few demanding words spewed from the mouths of the Bonvillian's, George decided to get a place of his own for his family, so he rented an apartment and moved out.

Dorothy wasn't nearly as ready as she thought she was to take on the responsibility of a wife and mother of a child. She became very homesick and distraught. She didn't like living away from her dad and mom, so the marriage only lasted a year because Dorothy took their child, Susan, and moved back home with her parents.

The Bonvillian's were not a bit bashful about telling George what they expected of him. They made it very clear that his responsibilities would be to pay child support, alimony, plus all the doctor and hospital bills. George didn't fight the Bonvillians. He was willing to meet every demand if he could, but this was a heavy burden for an immature young man to bear. This expectation became extremely rough on him, and he couldn't always find enough work to keep up.

Several times when George got behind on his child support, the Bonvillian's would have him thrown in jail. Finally, a friend advised George to join the Marines because the Marines would pay him enough money to satisfy his wife and her parents and give him enough money to live on.

George took the advice and joined the Marines.

CHAPTER FOUR

Marriage, Marines,
Music and Money

George was stationed at Camp Pendleton in San Diego, California. He began involving himself with some bad habits. He started smoking and drinking, and was also known to pick up a woman now and then. His former family life was all but a distant memory.

The worst thing that happened while George was in the Marines was that his most cherished singer, Hank Williams, Sr. died on January 1, 1953, and it devastated him. George absolutely loved Hank Williams and could not understand why he had to die at such a young age. Country Music suffered a great loss when Hank Williams died, but little did it know that there was another voice lurking for the opportunity to become another legend in its field. That voice belonged to George Jones and in due time, it would happen.

George served three years in the Marines. Although it wasn't what he really wanted out of life, he felt he was better off than trapped on a scaffold painting houses. He soon became preoccupied with his new way of life and lived it to the fullest. George never served active duty for which he was thankful and exited the Marines at last at the age of twenty-two.

It wasn't long after Hank Williams' death that George Jones came alive as a country singer. Maybe Country Music had realized its loss with the death of Hank Williams and wanted to replace Hank with someone as near to Hank's caliber as it could. That person could only be George Jones. As a young boy, George dreamed about someday getting to sing on the stage of the Grand Ole Opry. Of course at that time it was like fantasizing a fairy tale coming true. Everybody loved George's picking and singing, but those around him never thought he'd be any more than a honky-tonk singer. It was hard for the people who knew him to visualize this poor shy country boy ever making it to the limelight.

Folks had experienced the hard and drab times the Great Depression brought them. They were ready for a more lively and pleasurable life. Money was not so scarce as it had been a few years back, so now they had a little extra cash to spend on something they wanted such as the music they cherished. A market had opened up in the music industry, and the opportunity was wide open for George Jones. George was ready and willing. It was the love of his life, plus he needed the extra money it would provide for him. George was full of desire, determination, and had the talent. All he needed was an open door, and he could bust the music industry wide open.

The music business had just begun to blaze like a raging fire sweeping across the nation. Hank Williams, Roy Acuff, Bill Monroe, Ernest Tubb, and others had provided their style of music, but people were ready for something a little more lively and upbeat. What could be more exciting than to turn the radio on and hear Elvis Presley singing, *"You Ain't Nothing But A Hound Dog"* or *"Jailhouse Rock?"* Jerry Lee Lewis woke up everybody with his, *"Whole Lotta Shakin' Going On."* One artist after another was releasing hit records. People loved it! George Jones came on the scene with *"White Lightnin'"* and *"Why Baby Why."*

A lot of music was being created in Memphis, Tennessee at Sun Records, but it was happening all over the nation and rapidly spreading all over the world. The time was right for George Jones to make his break. He was out of his marriage, out of the Marines, and ready to go big time into music and money. He just needed that special someone to believe in him. Little did George know that he was about to meet the man who would introduce him to the world.

This man would believe in him whole-heartedly and would stick with him through thick and thin. George was about to meet that special someone who would lead him into becoming a country music legend. His name was Pappy Daily from Houston, Texas. He was a producer and owner of a record label and publishing company and was looking for someone to produce. He found what he wanted in George Jones.

CHAPTER FIVE

··

Pappy Daily
(Founder of George Jones)

George had worked the honky-tonks and barrooms but barely made enough money to survive. He was ready for something bigger and better, and he certainly deserved it. He desperately needed a record under his belt, so that his music could be heard beyond the streets of Beaumont and bars. Without a record deal, he would never be more than a local singer entertaining a bunch of half-drunk people and barely making a living. George was a gifted professional and needed to be heard. He wanted more than anything in the world to spend the rest of his life making music. It was his obsession that drove him, and George honestly never cared about stardom or even the money attached to it. If he could make an honest living and be able to live out his passion, he would be a happy man.

The big break George wanted so badly came when Pappy Daily and Bill Starnes founded STARDAY Records. Pappy heard George sing and loved his music, and George was exactly the singer he needed to bring into his new company. He signed George to his first record label that would begin a new career and way of life.

Country Music was rising in popularity, but Rock and Roll was raging across the Nation like wildfire. It was selling like crazy and being played on nearly every radio station. George felt he would have a better chance at success in Rock and Roll, so he made the decision and cut a deal with Pappy Daily, who produced George's first two songs.

"The Rocket" and *"Dad Gummit, How Come It"* were cut

and released under the name of Thumper Jones. George's middle name is Glenn, and Patterson is his mother's maiden name, so he also recorded under the pseudonym of Glen Patterson. There had been no success on his first releases, so he tried again but this time with a country song, *"There Ain't No Money In This Deal"* which was virtually a flop that did nothing for him but make him miserable. After three failed songs, Pappy Daily did not give up his confidence in George, so he gambled again and released *"Why Baby Why."* It was a hit!

George's next release was another flop and came about the time everybody thought he had finally made the big time. Many of George's peers felt like he was trying to sound too much like Hank Williams, Sr., who was no doubt his idol. It was Pappy Daily who turned things around when he told George that there had already been a Hank Williams, and now we need a George Jones. Pappy encouraged George to sing like himself and to develop his own style.

George took Pappy's advice and began to sing with his own inward feelings and developed a voice and style unlike anyone had ever heard. He was doing exactly what Pappy wanted of him, and Pappy was pleased with the unique phrasing and the pure soul that poured from George's vocal cords behind his clenched teeth. George had developed a method of singing that was far different from all the rest. This unique style was the tool George needed for real success and when George began to deliver the true George Jones with his voice, he began to succeed as an artist, who would eventually distinguish himself as the top singer in the world of Country Music.

Pappy Daily did more for George than jumpstart his amazing career. He took the shyness from George and built up his self-confidence. No one knew for sure what was to come in the after years, but Pappy kept on producing hit after hit for George and allowed him to keep gaining the ground that would make him the Country Music legend he is today.

....

CHAPTER SIX

Shirley Corley - Wife Number Two

The hit, *"Why Baby Why"* created a demand for George Jones, so he formed a band and hit the road. While playing a gig in Houston, Texas, George met a pretty young lady by the name of Shirley Corley. She was working as a carhop at a little drive-in restaurant, and George immediately was attracted to her although she was only eighteen years old and newly graduated from high school. Shirley was as attracted to George as he was to her, so they dated for a short time and then George asked Shirley to marry him. Shirley had no intentions of marrying George and kept turning him down; even though, he kept coming back and asking her again and again. Shirley admitted that she loved George but refused to commit because she was uncomfortable with his drinking.

Shirley was raised in church and had been taught to keep away from anyone who had the habit of drinking. Shirley loved George and desperately wanted to marry him, so she finally relented, tossed her beliefs aside, and the drinking didn't stop her. She felt that she could influence George to stop drinking if she married him. George and Shirley married in 1954.

George and Shirley were happily married until drinking became a problem. Shirley had been afraid this might happen because George never totally gave alcohol up no matter how much she encouraged him to do so. Shirley believed George was a really good man, and she so desperately wanted the marriage to work.

George, like many successful music stars, was on the road

touring and completing his show schedules. This started to become a problem with Shirley because there wasn't enough time being spent together for them to develop a good family life and share their love for each other.

George was conflicted between the love for his wife and home and the music business. George didn't want to lose his marriage, and he understood the demands on an artist the business makes when a talented person has chosen that profession. To be successful, he had to make numerous appearances in order to satisfy the expectations of his record label and his fans, which in turn results in record sales. He knew what he had to do, and he would have to do it regardless of the pressures it put on his marriage.

The time apart was especially hard on Shirley. The situation got complicated when Shirley discovered she was pregnant. George and Shirley were living with a member of George's family, and she was struggling between her emotions of George being gone all the time and juggling the problems of living with somebody else's relatives. The pressure on Shirley was heavy, and something had to give.

George decided the best thing was to take Shirley on the road with him. Shirley enjoyed this arrangement because she got to spend a lot of time with her husband but not for long. Jeffrey Jones was born in 1955 just before George became a huge star in Country Music, and Shirley had to return home to take care of the baby.

George was playing in honky-tonks, bars, and clubs, but the big stands had so far eluded him and so had the big paydays. Oddly, it was Shirley who encouraged George to do more professional shows. She recognized his talent could take him beyond the path he was pursuing. Shirley reasoned with George that if he was going to commit his life to his music, he needed a bigger stage to play. George realized Shirley was right.

He landed a spot on the Louisiana Hay Ride. All the major artists were doing shows there. Shirley attended many of George's shows but started becoming critical of how he was performing. Pappy Daily wanted to boost George's self-confidence realizing that he would never become the entertainer he could be if he didn't have the confidence he needed. Shirley was innocently undermining George's confidence in his work, and the criticisms only hurt his feelings and made him withdraw even more.

George was putting his career in front of his marriage, and this was causing some difficulties for Shirley to cope. At one time, she had thoughts that George was seeing other women and had no time for her; especially, when George got more and more involved with alcohol. Shirley realized she was not happy and in a bad situation, but she resolved to stick it out because of their son. Her decision to stay with her marriage ended up being a good one because soon after she found out she was pregnant. There were no more thoughts about ending the marriage, and their second son, Brian, was born in 1958.

The birth of Brian brought closeness between George and Shirley that had been lacking for a long time. Things were genuinely changing between the two of them. They began to show a lot more love and concern for each other, and Shirley had new hopes that their marriage would survive. George seemed to be happier being at home than he'd ever been; he even laid off drinking and was settling into a peaceful family life.

This happy arrangement didn't last long. George's desire to be on the road drew him away from his family once again, and he dragged the boozing habits with him. He was staying away from home for long periods of time leaving Shirley to care for the boys and manage the business.

George was making money and providing a good living for his family, but sometimes it is hard for the spouse of a successful entertainer to understand the rigors of dealing with promoters, the band, and a terrible load of hard work. Shirley couldn't deal with the fact that George was fused to the only way he would make a living the rest of his life, and the love he had for his music wasn't going to change.

In 1956, George had another hit record, *"What am I*

Worth?" After that release, he departed STARDAY and signed with Art Talmage of Mercury Records. He retained Pappy Daily as his producer and in 1957, Pappy produced another big hit, *"Don't Stop the Music."* It landed in the top twenty on the billboard charts. Shortly afterwards, he had another hit record, *"Too Much Water."* In 1958, he had great success with three more releases, *"Color of the Blues," "Treasure of Love,"* and *"If I Don't Love You."* George was on a roll of big hits that didn't stop. In 1959, he shot the moon with his first number one hit record, *"White Lightning."* The same year he released, *"Who Shot Sam?" "Big Harlan Taylor,"* and *"Money to Burn."*

In 1960, he released a wonderful song that he wrote himself, and it stayed on the charts for nine months, *"Window Up Above."* In 1962, he released the timeless number one hit, *"She Thinks I Still Care"* along with six other releases that made the charts. He released three songs in 1963 and in 1964 *"The Race Is On,"* and five more. George released six songs in 1965 and three more in 1966. The endless flow of hits one after the other was proof that George Jones had finally become successful at what he loved to do more than anything else in the world.

George had not forgotten the struggles he had experienced living in The Big Thicket, and how hard it was for him to get his first guitar. He had not forgotten how hard it had been painting houses for a few dollars to support a wife and child. He had not forgotten what it felt like to be thrown in jail for not being able to pay his child support, nor had he forgotten how hard it was to find odd jobs just to survive by the skin of his teeth. These are the reasons why he could not quit.

George Jones's career path found him first singing on the streets of Beaumont, shining shoes, singing in churches and revival meetings, singing in honky-tonks and bars, working as a disc jockey, painting houses, joining the Marines, back to singing with Eddie and Pearl at the Beaumont Playground, performing at the Louisiana Hay Ride, signing with STARDAY Records, touring on the road, signing with Mercury Records, leaving Mercury Records, signing with United Artists Record Label, and producing hit after hit after hit. He would truly become the King of Country Music. George Jones is a name that will be known throughout the world forever, and a major part of the credit belongs to a man who believed in him as a singer. The other part of the credit for George becoming a superstar stems from the encouragement and confidence his second wife, Shirley Corley Jones, instilled in him.

....

CHAPTER SEVEN

A Man Can Be a Drunk, But a Drunk Can't Be a Man

George had a serious drinking problem that he could not let go. He depended on alcohol to help him in many ways and used it for his own personal reasons. Alcohol gave him self-confidence and helped him overcome shyness. Many people who didn't know George could not comprehend that he could be a shy person, but he was. Alcohol gave him the courage to feel and do whatever he wanted.

Sometimes when George would be drinking, he was actually fun to be around. He would play his guitar and sing for hours on end. He loved to carry on with foolishness when he was in a jolly mood, and he'd do something crazy and just die laughing at himself. He'd laugh and talk about funny embarrassing things that he had experienced. He loved to tell tales about silly things that happened to other artists and got a lot of enjoyment sharing those experiences with the people around him.

George's drinking could also put him in a melancholy mood, and he would soothe himself by singing sad songs. Many times when George was singing those sad songs, he would cry. Those times made me think that even though George was a big star, he hurt inside just like everybody does, and he needed to be loved and not criticized. Drunk or sober, I could sit and listen to George sing for hours.

George found a crutch in alcohol. It helped him to toss all his worries and troubles aside and let his hair down. George was sensitive when he felt someone was "picking" on him and criticizing him for no good reason. He did not have a hard time setting someone straight if he felt this way; especially, if he thought the person was being cocky and smart with him. He could even become really angry and even a little vicious if you pushed him far enough. I didn't experience this side of George very often when he was drinking, but the few times I did was enough to let me know it was best to not tease him or pick on him when he was under the influence. He would never start an argument or get testy with anyone as long as he was left alone. If not, he would let someone know quickly to back off, or he would have nothing else to do with the person.

The worst time to be around George was when he was drunk and hacked off at someone. That's when you'd just better let him have his way, let him say whatever he wanted, listen well, and agree with him until he was finished letting off his steam. George was always right. If a person understood this about him, he could wind up in George's good graces and become his friend.

A person needed to know George well if he was going to be with him when he was drunk; otherwise, he could be very difficult to handle. He would do whatever popped in his head, and it was best to let him do exactly that, or you might find yourself facing some serious consequences.

Drinking made George prone to do outrageous things and get himself in hot water. He would often find himself the subject of a sensational story in a tabloid, magazine, or newspaper, and sometimes he'd wind up in jail.

An example of this behavior was a time when George's father became very sick, was admitted to the hospital, and not expected to live. George went to Texas to be with him in case his condition got worse. During the time his dad was sick, George got drunk. He began to recall some bad memories of his dad. He talked about times when the elder Jones had not treated his mom the way he should have. He recalled the times his dad would wake him up at night and make him sing to him. He became angry and spouted off these repressed feelings to his sick father. Some of the family members were very upset at George for acting the way he did at such a difficult time. George couldn't handle the stress of the circumstances, and his family didn't know George well enough to understand this. His reaction was the only way he knew to relieve the suffering he was experiencing. George had found himself faced with yet another situation he barely knew how to handle. Again, he turned to the bottle for help.

George had his own way of expressing his concern, his love, and his compassion. George's dad was also a heavy drinker, and that no doubt played a big role in the fact that George and his dad were not very close. George really loved his mother, and sometimes Mr. Jones had mistreated her. George had not forgotten it.

A drunken person can do a lot of damage to the feelings of someone else, and repairing the damage is very hard to fix. It's like the song, *"A Man Can be a Drunk, but a Drunk Can't be a Man."* In other words, don't expect a drunken man to do what a sober man would do. George was a person who didn't always display his true feelings. He might give you a real chewing out but love you to pieces at the same time. So, George got drunk sometimes. Whoop! What would you do if you were wearing his shoes?

Some of George's major frustrations happened during times when he'd record a certain song he loved and would want it for a single release. That song wouldn't get released because someone liked another song better. The chosen song wouldn't become a hit for George, and that would frustrate him to his core.

A good example of something George got upset about was when Tammy Wynette and he would record a number one hit record. It would stay number one on the billboard charts for weeks. The radio stations would play the fire out of it; it would be the talk of the town all over Nashville, and everyone just knew it would be "Song of the Year." George and Tammy would attend the Country Music Awards believing they would receive an award, but the honor would elude them. George would be extremely angry and disappointed.

George was always happy for the person who would win a Country Music Award, but it wasn't a time when George would want to go home and play a game of checkers. Most likely, there would be another night of pure misery for those around him.

Most things George did when he was drinking wouldn't have been done if he were sober, but not all of the things he did while drinking were wrong. There are a number of deeds he did while under the influence that were actually good. Sometimes, he'd give money away to someone he felt needed it. When you have a heart to help someone out, you can hardly call that a stupid thing although some people did call George's generosity stupid. It's a good thing. To be fair, George would give money to people in need when he was sober as well. He was good to everyone who would let him. He would do anything he could to help people whether he knew them or not. George was a generous man.

One of the best examples of George's generosity was when he built his mother and father a house. He passionately wanted them to own a house of their own, and so before they died, he built them a new home. George's parents were so proud of their new house, and Mr. Jones was so touched by what George had done that he nearly quit drinking. George's mom and dad mended their differences with their famous son, and became closer to each other than they had been in years.

Mr. Jones had always loved Gospel Music. A year or so before Mr. Jones died he had begun attending church and confessed to becoming a Christian. On September 7, 1967, just five days before George's thirty-sixth birthday, Mr. Jones passed away. I firmly believe that George building a house for his dad and mom had an impact on Mr. Jones making a change for the better in his life. God works in mysterious ways.

Shortly after Mr. Jones passed away, George made some changes in his own life. He quit working with Pappy Daily and moved to Nashville in an effort to keep his career going. It was 1967 and in that same year, he recorded a hit, *"When the Grass Grows Over Me."* In 1968 he had another hit, *"I'll Share my World With You."* George's success in Country Music seemed to have no end. There's no doubt in my mind that God was forever blessing him for his willingness to share his blessings with others. George had never been selfish; he'd always been willing to share a portion of what he had to help make someone else's life a little better. What a heart!

CHAPTER EIGHT

....

Melba Montgomery, Duet Partner

Melba Montgomery is my sister-in-law. George was working with United Artists when he met Melba and instantly they hit it off and discovered they had the perfect combination of voices. George loved Melba's voice so much that he convinced Pappy Daily to sign her with United Artists so that he could sing duets with her. Melba was working with Roy Acuff at the time and was living with Roy and Mildred at their home in Nashville.

George was living in Texas, and he wanted to meet with Melba, so he and Pappy drove the long trip to Nashville. They rented a room at Capital Park Inn. Melba had written a song she thought they might like as a duet, so she met them at the hotel and sang her song, *"We Must Have Been Out of Our Minds."*

George and Pappy loved it and within a couple of days, they were in the studio recording. United Artists released the song, and it became a huge hit for George and Melba. The song succeeded as the best selling song of the year and is still one of the greatest country duet classics of all time.

George and Melba first met when Melba was working The Grand Ole Opry with Roy Acuff. After the show one night, Melba went with Roy over to Tootsie's Orchid Lounge, and George was there. Melba said George was "juiced" on Jack Daniels, and she never saw him again until Pappy Daily called for her to sign with United Artists.

George and Melba had a lot in common and were a great

team. Both were raised in large poor families of talented musicians and singers. They loved telling stories of their childhood upbringing. They were both talented and very "countrified." George called Melba "Melber" because she had a pronounced country drawl that kept her from ever hiding her roots. George loved the way she talked, and the fact she was plain and simple and never changed attracted him to her. They loved being together and continued singing until 1967 after they had released seven duet records.

George and Shirley's marriage was barely holding together. George was drinking heavily, and Shirley resented the drinking plus the fact he was never home and abdicated the responsibility of raising Jeffrey and Brian and put the burden on her. By this time, Shirley had become so bitter toward George that she barely had a kind word for him when he was at home.

In 1970, George bought a nice home in Vidor, Texas. He was doing well financially and buying the house had put a little spark back in their marriage. Shirley had patiently waited for a time when she could be happy again. She felt the marriage was getting more stable and finally looked promising.

Shirley and the boys felt like the success of George's hit records was at last paying off for them and would change their lives for the better. Sadly, the new happiness didn't last because George started drinking heavily again, and Shirley was under a lot of stress and disappointment. She gave up on George ever quitting his drinking, or at least getting it under control, so she felt that all the peace and happiness she had hoped for was gone.

George was becoming wealthy, so he decided to open a restaurant in Vidor and named it George Jones Chuckwagon. He leased a building from a man named J.C. Arnold. Shirley and J.C. became friends through this arrangement, and as Shirley complained to him about George's drinking problems and staying on the road all the time, J.C. began feeling sorry for her. J.C. recognized the loneliness that Shirley was experiencing, and she began to rely on J.C. for consoling. Eventually, the friendship grew into a relationship.

George's arrangement with Melba Montgomery had grown far beyond a recording partnership. George liked Melba as a person and loved her disposition. Melba was young, single, talented, fun to be around, and extremely attractive. Melba's brother, Cranston, was a recording artist. Her other brother, Carl Montgomery, was a successful songwriter and wrote a hit recorded by Dave Dudley, *"Six Days on the Road,"* that became a country classic. Melba's brother, Aaron, worked with Hank Williams, Sr.

Earl "Peanutt" Montgomery is Melba's most famous brother. In addition to the songs Peanutt wrote for George and Melba as a duet, he also wrote many songs that Melba recorded as a solo artist. Peanutt is best known for the songs he wrote for George Jones. He wrote, *4033, Ship of Love, Where Grass Won't Grow* and many more that George recorded. Gene Pitney, George Jones, Tammy Wynette, Emmy Lou Harris, and Tanya Tucker are just a few of the many country stars that have recorded Peanutt's songs.

The entire Montgomery Family has been involved with music at the professional level and as you can see, many of them became famous. Melba's father, Fletcher Montgomery, taught music in churches when the kids were young, and he worked a moonlight job calling square dances. Melba's mother, Willie Mae Montgomery, played the mandolin. Melba's parents were playing and singing at an old fashioned cake walk when they met, so all the Montgomery children were born with natural talents inherited from their parents. The music connection with Melba all the way back to her upbringing was a turn on to George.

George loved Mr. and Mrs. Montgomery, and he would travel often with Melba to Florence, Alabama to visit her parents. Mrs. Montgomery would always have a table full of good old country cooking. There was nothing George liked any better than good country "fixings" as he called it. Mrs. Montgomery related to me many times how much she enjoyed watching George eat her cooking. She loved George and told stories about him until the day she died.

Shirley suspected for a long time there was a relationship

between Melba and George involving them in more than recording duets. She was not wrong. George and Melba were in love with each other, but this relationship had nothing to do with the cracking foundations of George and Shirley's marriage. They were headed for divorce regardless of George's affair with Melba.

Shirley and George each had found a mutual interest in someone else. A rumor was spreading that George Jones shot J.C. Arnold in the rear end when he found out about Shirley's affair with J.C. I asked George about that tale, and he told me that he "did no such thing." I believe George because if he'd gotten upset enough to shoot somebody, he sure wouldn't have cared to admit it. George was never physically mean to Shirley. His abuse stemmed from the neglect of Shirley and the boys, and he destroyed things that were expensive or had sentimental value when he got drunk. These actions by George made it hard for her to cope. She had sacrificed so much for George, and she really wanted to help him. She loved him dearly but didn't know what to do with him.

George was not ultra-insensitive to the cares of Shirley and the boys. He bought a home in Florida, so they would have a place to retreat from everything and everybody. He and Shirley hoped the new location would give them more time together, and Shirley thought it could help them work things out. It turned out to be wishful thinking. The situation ended up being volatile, and the changes revealed it was too late for them to mend the sore feelings they had for each other. George continued to drink. Shirley began to feel that there was no hope and no need in trying to hold on to George and keep the marriage going. She finally mentioned divorce to George. It was a sore subject, but he gave in, and they divorced in 1968.

Shirley was a classy lady, and I admired her. She had a great disposition and was quite brilliant. She is to be praised for the care she gave to George's sons, Jeffrey and Brian. She was a great mother to both. George and Shirley were married for fourteen years when they came to an amicable divorce settlement. George paid child support for his two sons. Shirley took possession of the house in Vidor, Texas, and George received a second ranch house they owned in Vidor plus the Florida house and its contents. He later bought a tour bus with the money from the sale of the Vidor property. George gave Shirley a generous cash settlement, and she wanted George's income from royalties for the benefit of the boys. George generously complied with her request as part of the settlement. Once all terms of the divorce were met, George and Shirley entered into their separate lives. Shirley eventually married J.C. Arnold, and they were together until his death. I believe that George loved and respected Shirley very much, but the demands from the music business took too much of his time and attention to properly maintain a good family life. George and Melba's relationship had no foundation and came to an end when George became involved with another female singer. Her name was Virginia Wynette Pugh; better known today as Tammy Wynette.

Melba Montgomery later married George's guitar player, Jack Solomon. They live in Nashville and have two daughters, Jackie and Melissa. Jackie is married to Blake Chancey, a producer, and Melissa is married to Shane Barrett who is also a producer, musician, and songwriter. Melba stays busy co-writing songs, and her husband, Jack, works as a rhythm guitar player on many of the recording sessions in Nashville. Melba still speaks highly of George, but she says her biggest fear in marrying George was his drinking. Melba maintains that George was very good to her, and he never harmed her in any way except it was emotionally stressful to worry about him keeping his bookings, and whether he would show up drunk or sober. She said there was no real mean streak in George that she ever knew or experienced. Although Melba never knew exactly what to expect from George, she understood him and deeply cared for him. Her favorite thing to say about George is: "That George was a mess."

CHAPTER NINE

Possum and Peanutt -
Two Peas in a Pod

George "Possum" Jones and Earl "Peanutt" Montgomery met when Melba Montgomery introduced George to her brother. They became instant friends and remained that way until George's death in April 2013. The similarities of how they grew up were a recipe that melded them into "brothers." Although neither of them was educated past grammar school, they both became very successful in the music business because of their unique gifts to write and perform country music. They also mirrored each other's lifestyles and shared the same nemesis. They were heavy drinkers. Through all their drunken sprees, wild living, and carousing, they were somehow able to do what they loved the most, and that was to sing, play, and write songs.

"Possum" became a legendary singer, and "Peanutt" became a legendary songwriter.

George and Peanutt grew to be inseparable. George once told Peanutt that if he loved him anymore than he did, they would be accused of being gay. Peanutt felt the same about George. They could not be any more committed to each other than they were through the majority of their lives. Peanutt served George, and George got whatever he wanted from Peanutt. Many times Peanutt would get out of bed at 3:00 a.m. and bail George out of jail. Sometimes George would get drunk and want to take off to Florida at midnight. Peanutt would pack up and go. Whenever they were drunk and traveling, I was the designated driver.

When Peanutt and George drank together, they usually played their guitars, sang songs, and wrote down lyrics to a new song they were composing. They would laugh, act like fools, and have a ball telling stories on each other. Alcohol seemed to have the same reaction on both of them. If George was in a good mood, he could be fun to be around. If he was in a foul mood, there was no fun being with him. He could be unpredictable. Peanutt was the same way, but they never got rowdy with each other, and one would always help the other out when either was caught in a difficult situation.

Peanutt wrote several of the songs George and Melba recorded. Peanutt and I were touring with Melba and George, so we were together all the time. Melba and I had our hands full trying to manage them. There were times when both of them would show up drunk and expect to entertain a crowd. Melba struggled during times like this, and it created a lot of stress for her because Peanutt, her guitar player, and George, her duet partner, were in no shape to do what they were supposed to do. Melba would be fit to be tied. She'd say, "I'm gonna beat the fire out of both of them after the show is over." Melba realized she had to do something about George's behavior because he influenced Peanutt. If she could control George, Peanutt would be no problem.

Melba began making private decisions about her relationship with George. She was trying to decide whether she could ever be happy carrying on a life like he would hand her. Melba finally pulled the plug on the relationship, and they parted ways, but her decision didn't affect the friendship or business relationship between George and Peanutt.

Melba still has a love for George. She respects him highly and will always hold him close to her heart, but she knew that if she married him, it would never last because she couldn't handle his drinking.

Peanutt had worked as a musician at the Grand Ole Opry. He was living in Nashville and was an exclusive songwriter for

Sure Fire Music Publishing Company. George was a writer for Glad Music Publishing Company. George wanted Peanutt to sign as an exclusive writer with Glad, which was owned by Pappy Daily, George's producer. The idea was for George and Peanutt to write songs together and be uninhibited by the conflict of two studios. This arrangement would give full publishing rights to Pappy Daily's company, and it did work out great for all three of them.

Peanutt toured with several of the Grand Ole Opry stars such as Cowboy Copus, Red Foley, the Willis Brothers, and many others. He played bass guitar, rhythm guitar, and the upright "Bull" bass. Few people know that Peanutt sang and toured with Michael Landon and Chase Webster. They were known as the "Ponderosa Trio."

Like other artists, Peanutt traveled extensively during the time he was touring. He was a regular on the USO tours with the Willis Brothers, and he played many shows with Judy Lynn at the Golden Nugget Casino in Las Vegas. Peanutt loved the road but also missed having his time with George. It was circa 1965 that Peanutt quit touring with the Grand Ole Opry stars. George Jones and Peanutt Montgomery hooked up again and began writing and recording even more songs since Peanutt wasn't bogged down with the rigorous travel schedule he had while touring.

I first saw Peanutt Montgomery at the Florence Armory in Florence, Alabama. He and his band were fronting a show for Jimmy Newman. I asked a friend of mine, Jewell Hines, to go with me to the concert. I didn't know anything about Peanutt or anybody else there; I just wanted to go to the show to have something to do. Jewell and I were sitting in the second row by the stage. When Peanutt got through playing, he walked off the stage, came straight to me, and asked me for a dance. I danced with him, and he kissed me while slightly biting my lip. I really didn't know just what to make of it, but I liked his boldness. We talked very little after the dance, and he returned to the stage. After the show was over, he found me again and asked me to join him for dinner. I refused by using the excuse that I already had other plans. Actually, I had no plans but because I didn't know him, I didn't want to go anywhere with him. I never thought any more about the man who danced with me.

After weeks had gone by, the Alabama State Fair came to Florence, Alabama. Another friend asked me to go to the fair with her, and I agreed to it. As it turned out, Peanutt was at the fair, and he knew the girl I was with. He had been the best man at Billy and Sue Kinnington's wedding and was a close friend of Sue's husband for years. Billy was a local musician but had played with Peanutt's band.

Peanutt asked Sue about me. Sue told him that I wouldn't be interested in him because I was already seeing someone. Peanutt didn't recognize me as the same girl he had danced with at the Jimmy Newman show, so he went on his way and said nothing more to Sue about me.

A couple of months passed. Jewell Hines and I needed something to do, so we were driving around Florence. I was living at the time with Jewell and her husband, Jimmy. Jimmy was out of town most of the time, so Jewell and I would get on the streets and drive around just for fun. On this particular evening while riding on Tennessee Street, Jewell and I noticed a 1964 blue Thunderbird occupied with two males that kept closely following my 1964 turquoise Ford Galaxy 500.

The T-Bird pulled up beside us; a window rolled down. "How about meeting us at Dusty Joe's?" one of them asked.

I answered tongue-in-cheek, "Why not?"

They sped off towards the popular sandwich shop, and we followed. On the way I told Jewell that if they ask us to go somewhere with them, I will refuse because I have no interest in either of them.

"Well, I kinda like that fellow that was on the passenger side," she said.

"Well, I didn't pay much attention, but I like the driver better myself," I replied.

Jewell was married, but she and her husband couldn't get along, so it wasn't much of a marriage. Jewell wasn't a person to sit at home alone while her husband was gone all the time. She was much older than me. I was only 18 years old, and she was in her 30's. She was redheaded, high tempered, and cute.

We sat with Peanutt and his brother, Monty, at Dusty Joe's. As predicted, they asked us to ride around with them, and I told them that I couldn't because I had to go to the laundry to get my clothes before they closed. Jewell wanted to take them up on the offer, but I flat refused. She glared at me.

"Maybe another time," Jewell said.

Peanutt wasted no time. "How about tomorrow?"

"I'll give you our phone number, and you can call us in the morning," she replied.

Peanutt called early the next morning, and I answered the phone.

"Is this that pretty little blonde I saw last night?' he jubilantly asked.

"This is Charlene, the blonde-headed girl who was driving," I answered.

"You're the one I'm interested in, and my brother likes the redhead. Are you going to see me today?"

"Yes, that's what Jewell wants us to do; she likes your brother."

"Just meet us at Dusty Joe's." He finished the conversation, and we hung up.

For whatever reason, Jewell and I agreed to ride around with the boys.

Peanutt wanted us to meet his mom and dad, Fletcher and Willie Mae Montgomery, and his sister, Melba. They were very nice to us. Mrs. Montgomery was in the kitchen cooking, Mr. Montgomery was watching TV, and Melba was sitting with her hair in rollers under a hair dryer. I had no idea who Peanutt and Melba Montgomery were except that Peanutt was a musician.

After we said our goodbyes and left the Montgomery home,

we drove up the Natchez Trace, walked on some nature trails, and then stopped at a rest area. There was a picnic table near a tree, and a limb was hanging over the table. I decided I wanted to take a swing from that limb. I climbed upon the table and started swinging, and I really didn't care what anybody thought about it because I was being who I am take it or leave it.

I had a good time with Peanutt and Monty. We talked all day. It didn't matter if either of them liked me because after this one day, I most likely wouldn't see them again. Late in the afternoon, I told Peanutt I needed to go home because I had a date that night.

"Okay," he said, but I noticed his mood changed. I asked him what was wrong?

"Oh, nothing," he answered quietly.

I thought it was so cute of him to pout because I had a date with someone else because he didn't even know me.

When we were nearly home, I told him the truth; I didn't really have a date. He wanted to know if he could take me out to dinner and a movie. I told him no, but he could come over to visit.

Peanutt accepted my offer, and we talked for about two hours while sitting in the living room. He asked me if I'd ride up to Nashville with him the next afternoon, and I told him I would. The next morning, I got up early and went to Kriesman's Clothing Store in Florence. I wasn't sure where we would be going in Nashville, so I wanted to be prepared. I purchased several items including a beautiful short black dress with rhinestone spaghetti straps and a matching handbag and shoes. I also bought a rhinestone studded black denim pantsuit. That's what I wore that day to Nashville.

Our first stop in Nashville was at Shot Jackson's house. Shot was dating recording artist, Donna Darlene, and Peanutt told them that he was going to take me to Tootsies Orchid Lounge. That sounded like a very sophisticated place, so I changed into my new dress and heels. Shot and Donna really complimented me about how I looked, but Donna made the comment:

"What you had on would have been good enough to wear to Tootsies. It's just a place where a lot of the stars hang and shoot the bull."

I didn't feel safe to change back into my denim pantsuit.

We left the Jackson's and went to Tootsies. Once there, my first thought was,

"Where does an orchid fit into this scroungy looking place?"

The lounge was quite a place. Names were written all over the walls, there were cobwebs hanging everywhere, and several drunken people were lounging in the booths. The smoke was so thick you could cut it with a knife.

Peanutt made reference to a man sitting in a booth at the rear of the lounge who was spouting off some very foul language,

"That's Faron Young in that back booth," Peanutt said, "Come on, I'll introduce you to him."

We walked over to the back where Faron Young was sitting, and Peanutt introduced him to me.

"Peanutt, you're picking them classy these days. This is the best looking damn woman in this place," Faron said. Peanutt only smiled and walked back to our table with me.

After Peanutt and I got home from Nashville, we never stopped seeing each other. He had captured my heart, and there was only one other piece of important unfinished business for him to do.

Peanutt couldn't wait to introduce me to George Jones. I knew who George was because my favorite song was, *"Window Up Above."*

Peanutt drove me to Nashville where George was recording one of Peanutt's songs. George wanted us to come to the Biltmore Hotel where he was staying. When we got to his room, I was surprised to see other people in the room with George. I was introduced to Jeannie Seely, Hank Cochran, and to George's heavy drinking. Pappy Daily, George's producer, was there. I remember exactly what George said when Peanutt introduced me to him.

"Hot-a-mighty-damn, what a set of legs!" George yelled.

"This is a low class, foul mouth, drunken, and moral-less bunch of business." I thought to myself. My introduction to these stars did not impress me. George was drunk, Faron Young was drunk, Tootsies was a dive, and Shot Jackson and Donna Darlene were living together.

Of course I was naïve; I had never been around clubs or musicians. This was all everyday stuff to Peanutt but a whole new world to me. Peanutt and I kept on dating. He was so nice to me and treated me with great respect. I was brought up in church and taught to stay away from people who drank alcohol, so I was distressed when I found out that Peanutt liked alcohol as much as George did. It was too late for me though because my feelings were too strong to toss him away.

George and Peanutt were such good men. I just could not understand why the alcohol was so important to them. Both of the men were such sweet and kind people. Why did they have to drink?

I liked Peanutt more than any man I'd ever dated, but I had been married before and even though Peanutt knew it, I hadn't told him the whole story. I was afraid if I did, it would break us up. I kept procrastinating telling him some important things about me I knew he would eventually find out. One afternoon, Peanutt called me out of the clear blue.

"Charlene, I want you to come over to Mother's tomorrow to have dinner with my family."

Okay," I replied.

The next day I showed up at The Montgomery's house. Melba and Mrs. Montgomery had prepared a big dinner for Peanutt and me. Peanutt had invited his brothers and their wives, so the entire Montgomery clan was there for dinner. I felt strange like something was up. After we finished eating, Peanutt said he wanted to say something.

"Charlene, this dinner was prepared for me and you," he said.

"Why?" I asked.

He reached in his coat pocket and pulled out this gorgeous engagement ring. "This is for you, I want to marry you."

I was thrilled out of my mind. I was in love with Peanutt. I knew I had never loved anybody as much as I did him in all of my life, but I had not let anybody know how I really felt because of the situation I was in. I thought it would all have to come to an end somewhere along the way. My first thought at the sight of the ring was, *"What do I do now?"* I accepted the ring. He placed it on my finger and kissed me with no hesitation in front of everybody. My eyes filled with moisture; I wanted to cry.

I needed to get alone and get some space where I could think. Peanutt got busy talking to his brothers and their wives, so I excused myself and left the room. I went to Peanutt's room to use the phone. I called Jewell to tell her how excited I was about the ring, and I intended to get some advice.

"Jewell, you've got to tell me what to do," I blurted as soon as she answered.

"What do you mean?"

"Peanutt has given me an engagement ring, and it's gorgeous. I am so happy because this is exactly what I hoped would happen."

"Have you told him about your situation yet?" Jewell knew I hadn't said a word about it.

"No," I answered.

"What are you going to do?" Jewell quietly asked.

"I'm going to get Peanutt to ride out to White's Lake with me, and I'm going to tell him everything. I'll give the ring back to him if he wants it."

"Are you going to tell Peanutt that you are pregnant and have been the whole time you've dated him?"

"Yes, I'll tell him that I was pregnant by Louis Hartzog, my husband, when I met him," I replied.

"Well, how in the world do you think he'll take this blow?" Jewell asked.

"I don't know. I just know that I love him, and I want to marry him. I should have told him in the very beginning, but I never thought we'd ever fall in love with each other."

"I think that's what you should do," Jewell said without quibbling.

"Okay, but it's going to kill me if he breaks up with me."

I let about an hour pass after Jewell and I hung up before I asked Peanutt to go for a ride with me. He told the family how much he appreciated them for coming and for preparing the meal for us. I thanked them also and tried my best to put on a happy face but inside, I was full of turmoil.

Peanutt and I drove out to White's Lake. Peanutt pulled up close to the water and turned off the motor.

"Peanutt," I began, "I love you more than you will ever know, but I have to give this ring back to you. Take it back to Zales and get your money back. I can't accept it, and I'm going to tell you why."

"There is something I've never told you about me, and now is the time I have to do it."

He stopped me and said, "You don't have to tell me; I already know you're pregnant."

"How can you possibly know that?" I asked.

"I heard you on the phone with Jewell. I listened in to find out what Jewell would say about the engagement ring."

I handed Peanutt the ring, and I cried.

"Is this what you want to do?" he asked.

"Yes it is. This is not fair to you, and I hate it that I didn't tell you earlier, but I didn't think we'd continue dating, and by the time I realized we cared for each other, I was afraid to tell you."

I then asked Peanutt to take me home. When we arrived at Jewell's house, Peanutt let me out of the car, and I told him I didn't want to see him again, ever. He said, "Okay" and drove away.

I cried for two straight weeks. I couldn't stop crying I was so messed up. I was divorcing my husband, Louis Hartzog, but I couldn't have the divorce finalized until after the baby was born because his insurance wouldn't pay for the pregnancy unless we were married.

When our divorce papers were signed, I was two months pregnant. I wasn't even showing when I met Peanutt. I had been dating Peanutt for four months, and I was six months pregnant when he gave me the engagement ring. I was still not showing. My pregnancy was a secret except for a handful of people who knew it. Louis, Jewell, and my doctor were the only people who knew this secret.

Two weeks passed, and I was lying on the couch when the phone rang.

"Charlene, this is Peanutt, and I'm coming over there. I don't care if you're pregnant with twins. I'm going to marry you anyway. I love you, and I'll love that baby just as much. I'll see you in a few minutes." He hung up without giving me a second to answer or rebut his comments.

Within minutes, Peanutt pulled in the driveway. He started unloading grocery bags from the car. He carried a bag from Kroger's, Kriesman's, and a drug store. He came in the house and sat the bags on the floor. He opened the Kroger Store bag first.

"I bought you some juice, fruit, raisins, and all kinds of healthy foods. I want you to begin eating this food and drinking the juice for your health and for the health of the baby."

He pulled up the bag from the drug store.

"Now, here are some vitamins for you to take and some lotion for your belly."

Then he went to the Kriesman's bag and pulled out two beautiful maternity outfits.

"These will look so good on you; I think they are so pretty," he commented.

The dresses were very cute and dainty looking. I couldn't wait to wear them. Peanutt was just as happy as I was and from that day forward, we never broke up again.

I went everywhere with Peanutt and the bigger I got, the prouder he was. I only gained fifteen pounds the whole time I was pregnant. I was always really slim and wore a size three before I got pregnant.

Peanutt had never been married, and it was neat that he wanted to take me to all his shows where he was playing music and wasn't ashamed of me. He had to do a show at the Sky Park Country Club, and I thought surely he wouldn't want to take me with him to that one, but he did. I wore one of the Kriesman's outfits he had bought for me, and he was so proud of me. He introduced me to everybody.

The last three months went quickly, and it was time for the baby to arrive. Peanutt waited anxiously day by day. We didn't know if the baby would be a boy or girl, but I was leaning for a girl, and Peanutt didn't care either way as long as the baby was healthy.

Peanutt got a call on April 1, and he had to go to Nashville for the day. On the way out the door he paused, turned towards me, and said:

"Do not get sick while I'm gone, I'll be back tonight."

Peanutt drove off, and I went outside to wash my car. When I finished, I looked around in a patch of clover. I found a four-leaf clover and put it in a glass of water. At this time, I was living with my sister, Nell Lee. I told Nell that I was going to have a girl because I found a four-leaf clover for good luck. I then got on the phone and called a couple of friends and told them that I was in the hospital and had the baby. I said it's a girl with blue eyes and blonde hair. They were thrilled for me. They had forgotten it was April 1st. I had to play this "April Fool's Day" joke. I was just having fun to pass the time while waiting for Peanutt to get back home.

It turns out this was not an "April Fool's" joke. I had gone out in the yard again and decided to turn a cartwheel. I was feeling good. It was a sunny day, and maybe I was feeling too good. By the time I went back into the house, I began to feel a little funny. My first thought was, *"I shouldn't have turned that cartwheel."* About that time, I felt water going all over my legs. I waited about two hours before I called my doctor because I had not felt any pain. My sister insisted that I call him.

"Dr. Bohannon, my water broke two hours ago; what do you want me to do?" I casually asked.

I went to the hospital at about 4:00 p.m. I still had no pain. Peanutt had not come home yet. I called Sue Kennington and told her to tell Peanutt as soon as he got home that I was in the hospital. My labor pains began about 6:00 p.m. The doctor came in and told me we were going to do a natural childbirth, and that the baby would be born breech. He said I would need all of my strength, and that he would give me something for pain. At 7:45 p.m. on April 1, 1966 the baby came. She was born with blue eyes, blonde hair, and weighed seven pounds and five ounces.

Peanutt came home at 8:45 p.m. and learned that I was in the hospital and had the baby. He didn't believe Sue. He thought she made it up to pull an "April Fool's" joke on him. He got in his car and took off to Sue's. When she told him I wasn't there, he looked in her closets, in her bathroom, under the beds, and all through her house still thinking it was a prank. He called my name the whole time he was looking for me. He finally realized it was not a joke and rushed to the hospital. He realized that the biological father would probably be there, so he waited downstairs in the lobby and sent Sue to my room to see who was with me. Louis was there but was about to leave.

Sue waited until he was gone and then told me Peanutt was in the lobby. I told her to ask Peanutt to go to the Chapel. When everyone was out of my room, I got out of bed and went to the Chapel. I saw Peanutt, and he was actually trembling. We spent about an hour in the chapel talking, and I told him everything that was discussed in the room with my ex-husband.

I didn't know that the nurses on my floor were searching everywhere for me. They had brought some medicine for me, and I was gone. A nurse in a triangle shaped, white cap came and told me to go back to my room.

"I'm not going back right now," I answered.

"I'll have to tell your doctor about this." she replied.

"Fine, but I'm staying here with him for a while longer."

Peanutt and I talked for a few more minutes, and then I went to my room. The nurses were pretty upset with me, but I didn't care. Peanutt went home but called me and talked for about two hours.

My mother was upset with me because during the birth of my baby, I kept asking for Peanutt. The doctor came out of the delivery room and said to my mother and Louis, "Somebody go get her some peanuts, that's all she keeps asking for."

The doctor didn't know anything about Peanutt, but he knew I was divorced from Louis. My mother and Louis knew what I was craving wasn't peanuts, and that irritated my mother. It didn't bother Louis because I had told him all about Peanutt.

Three days later, Peanutt came to the hospital to pick up the baby and me and took us to Bill and Sue Kennington's house. I stayed with Sue and Bill until I was able to return to my sister's. Peanutt came to see me every day. We named our little girl, "Teresa True Hartzog." The name Teresa came from a friend of Peanutt's who had died. Terry Thompson was a very good guitar player and singer and had been in a band with Peanutt. We got the name "True" from Dallas Frazier, who is a well-known songwriter and friend. Dallas had told us he thought "True" would be a pretty name for a girl, so we used that name.

The insurance company paid all the hospital and doctor bills, so the divorce was final on July 12, 1966. Peanutt and I married on July 22, 1966. We rented a cute little apartment in Florence. We furnished it and made a nursery for True. Peanutt loved shopping for baby clothes, and he spent a ton of money on that baby. He bought a baby bed, stuffed animals, rattles, and all kinds of pretty little baby things. Peanutt kept his word. He loved True and took care of her as if she was his very own.

Peanutt had not been drinking very much during the

pregnancy mainly because he was spending most of his time with me. We didn't have any real problems until some of his old friends started coming around. When he started drinking more, I knew it was the influence of those relationships. I was going to do something about this, so I started calling them out, one by one. I threatened them with calling the police and turning them in if they tried to pass Peanutt a pill of some kind. They knew I meant business. Peanutt would get mad at me for this, but I just didn't care. I felt I was doing the right thing for his sake. Finally, I got him interested in fishing and hunting. I'd go with him, and we'd spend every day on the river fishing and cooking out. We had fun. His dad started going with us and he loved to fish. We'd spend days away from home, and no one could bother us. When Peanutt got tired of fishing, I introduced him to arrowhead hunting, and he got hooked on it. We'd go hunt arrowheads all day. Sometimes, we'd go thirty or forty miles away and find some real nice fields to hunt arrowheads. We really enjoyed that.

Arrowhead hunting, fishing, and hunting eventually had to be replaced by other interests, so Peanutt became fascinated with flying radio-controlled airplanes. He loved this hobby most of all. Every time we'd go to Nashville, he would have to stop in Hobby World and get a new airplane to build. They were very expensive, and it took a lot of time to build one. He'd spend days in our basement building his planes. Peanutt was totally content flying airplanes, and it saved a ton of heartache for me.

George Jones and Peanutt Montgomery were exactly alike in this way. They both had to be kept occupied doing something they liked to keep them away from alcohol, and I did a good job minding their business. Idle time was not a good time for either of them. It was when they had idle time that they would drink.

We moved from the apartment and after three more moves, we ended up in a house on Hough Road in Florence, Alabama. While we were living on Hough Road, Peanutt began to increase his drinking habit. I told him that I wanted him to get a job. Although he didn't like the idea, he realized he needed something to keep him occupied. He applied for a job at Reynolds Metal Company where my dad worked, but they turned him down because he told them he had never had a job in his life. They must have thought at 26 years old, he was getting a very late start. He applied for a job at the steam cleaning company, and they hired him. His first job steam cleaning was at a house where a bad water leak had soiled the carpet. He lasted half a day. When he got home he announced he didn't like the job, so he quit. That was the last job he applied for. I thought we could work together and build a business, so I went to the Electrolux Vacuum Cleaner Company and applied for jobs. They hired both of us. We went to work selling vacuum cleaners. Electrolux makes superior vacuum cleaners, and we outsold every agent in the company for three weeks. We sold to all of our relatives, friends, and a few outsiders. Then we quit. Our boss did not want to see us go, but we were finished.

We decided to move again. We bought a cute little three-bedroom one-bath house on Shade Avenue in North Florence. Peanutt was going to have to get busy and write some songs if we were going to pay for that house. I look back now, and I don't know how on earth we made it. We had a new truck, a new car, a house, nice furniture, and no job. I wonder sometimes how we made it on Peanutt's royalties. Back in those days royalties weren't as much as they are today. The Good Lord watched over us.

I had always refused to move to Nashville. It took seven years of marriage to get me to move there, but we kept on writing songs. I got a job at Kmart and worked in the stationery department. I loved the job, but I didn't stay there long because Melba wanted Peanutt to go to New York on a show date she was booked for, and I wanted to go with them. Peanutt told me I couldn't go because I had a job. I told him that by the time Melba and he were ready to go, I wouldn't have a job because I was going to quit and go with them.

I went to New York with Peanutt and Melba. Melba performed at the Nashville Club on the bottom floor of the Taft Hotel.

I enjoyed the show, and I enjoyed the trip. I never worried about that job. I went back to Kmart, and my boss rehired me. I worked for a couple of months and quit again, so I could go on the road with Peanutt and Melba fulltime.

The only other job I ever had was at Barbers Cafeteria in Florence. I lasted about two months. Peanutt picked me up when I got off work and one night when he came, he was drinking. I made up my mind right then that I would never work another job, and I never did go back to work.

Peanutt was writing a lot and doing well by getting some real good cuts by various artists. Tanya Tucker, Beau (her father), her sister La Costa, and her mother Juanita came to stay with us for quite a while. They were trying to get in the music business in Nashville. They were introduced to John Capps who owned the K-Ark Records label in Nashville. John turned Tanya down because she was only nine years old.

Peanutt and Ron Ballew cut a record with La Costa at Widget Studio in Sheffield, Alabama. La Costa recorded an old tune entitled, *"I Will,"* but nothing became of it. Tanya, Peanutt and I wrote a commercial for Sealy Mattress Company and presented it to Kelso Herston. He liked it, but we never got paid. Tanya and I wrote a song together called, *"I Just Dropped By to See if I Was Really Gone."* Someday we need to do something with that song.

George and Peanutt loved music more than they loved anything or anybody. They loved the bottle, and neither cared about the consequences of drinking until they screwed up. Peanutt and George never got into a fuss or fight when they were drinking together. They would just cut up and act crazy. They'd dress up in overalls and a white shirt and do some crazy old songs and laugh at themselves. They didn't hurt anybody or fight with people and usually their shenanigans happened at home and were harmless.

Sometimes we'd invite some special friends over, but I wouldn't put up with anything off-color, and I was very choosy about who I invited into my home. I knew George would be safe at our house, and I wouldn't let anybody take advantage of him. When he came over to drink, I'd make him count his money and sign a paper showing we had counted it, and then I made him give it all to me. I meant it when I said that no one in my home was going to take advantage of George Jones.

George had his strange quirks. Out of the clear blue, he would want to take off to places in Florida or take a cruise somewhere. Peanutt and I would go with him and on most of the trips, he'd want to come back by the time we got to where we were going. He would suddenly sober up and change his mind.

George wasn't mean when he was drunk; he laughed and talked a lot. He'd pick and sing and make me name the tune. He'd play old songs that he thought I wouldn't know, but most of the time I knew them. He was not vicious unless somebody was teasing him the wrong way, and he thought someone was trying to get to him. I've seen him chew a few people out, but it was because he noticed something about them that he didn't like. Even when George was drunk, it was difficult to pull one over on him. He was wise to people. I liked it when he put people in their places; especially, when they deserved it.

George had a mind of his own. He did what he wanted when he wanted, and he didn't care what anybody thought of it. Peanutt was very much the same way. I recall one time when Peanutt was working with the Willis Brothers shortly after we were married. He went to Frankfurt, Germany, and I wouldn't go with them because I didn't want to fly. When they had been there a few days, Peanutt went to the show with the Brothers. He forgot and left the windows open in his hotel room. When he returned, he found pigeons had defecated on virtually everything in his room. Peanutt was beyond aggravated, and he was homesick, so he did what he always did. He drank a few beers, and then he called me.

"Charlene, I miss you, and I'm leaving here and coming home."

He jumped in a cab to the airport and flew home. The Willis Brothers missed him, so Guy Willis called me.

"Charlene, we can't find Peanutt, have you heard from him?"

"Yes, he's on his way home," I replied.

"That little snot head," Guy complained, "He's supposed to work with us tonight." Guy just burst out laughing. He knew Peanutt, and he knew that if Peanutt got restless, he'd go home.

"Charlene, I knew you should have come with us."

The alcohol mixed with the music business sometimes became a real problem to me. Music was our way of making a living, and the drinking seemed to bind up the work that needed to be done. In the early years of working in Nashville, we would all stay at the Biltmore Hotel with George and Pappy Daily. Peanutt and I would drive up to Nashville to meet George and Pappy to pick out the songs for George's session. Most of the time, it would be set for 2:00 p.m. the next day. By the time we'd get to Nashville, George would be high as a kite, and Peanutt would be pretty well lit, too. I'd think: *How in the devil are they going to know what's a good song and what isn't?* Pappy was always there, and he would select the songs that he liked.

Sometimes George would be very upset about something and wouldn't even go to the studio to record. Pappy would have to send somebody else into the studio to use the time in place of George. Other times when George would arrive at the studio, he would be drunker than Rooster Brown trying to chase down nine hens. Somehow they managed to decipher the bad songs from the good that Peanutt wanted them to hear, and George would go in and record the sessions.

It was always harder on the studio musicians than anyone. It made the session a little more difficult to get finished. There were times when the musicians would get the tracks laid down, and George would go back and "dub over" his voice on the track at a later date.

I really and truly liked George from the first day I met him. I didn't care about him because he was a star; I didn't give a rip about that. I never have been a star struck person. I like people for what I see in them, for their character, and not for their social status in the world. I could feel for George. I overlooked his drinking even though I hated the thought of him drinking alcohol. I don't know why it was different with George; he was the only person that I would tolerate drinking around Peanutt. I resented everybody else that drank. I saw something beneath the alcohol in George. I was sympathetic toward him. I can't really explain it, but what George did when he was drinking was different from all the rest of Peanutt's friends. For one thing, I could tell that George liked me. I didn't think George would do anything that would hurt me. I knew he wasn't trying to get Peanutt to do things against me, and George never seemed to mind my being with Peanutt and him. Most of Peanutt's other friends would try to get Peanutt away from me. They seldom ever succeeded because I would run them off and tell them to never come back around. I didn't trust anybody; especially, if the person drank. I trusted George more than anybody I knew in the business.

Peanutt and George were good men at heart. They were like brothers and were loyal to each other. It was a true friendship, and I cherished that. George was good to me. He always respected me, and that meant everything to me. Our friendship was one that is very hard to find, and I will always miss it.

I want to set the record straight that even though I hate alcohol and have expressed my opinion pretty graphically, George and Peanutt weren't drinking all the time. We had a lot of fun, and none of us had to go to a job each day. We had nothing but time to kill, and we killed it by doing whatever we felt like doing.

It didn't matter where George and Peanutt were going as long as I could go. They were not about to go anywhere together without me, and everybody knew it. That's how we were. We did everything together, and that's why we were together for thirty years.

George and Peanutt were good writers, musicians, singers, and they made a lot of money doing what they loved, but they also enjoyed living a common life. They loved the simple things. They honestly didn't care about money, but they loved spending it. They loved antique cars, and they loved going into business. They were never afraid of taking chances, and they would venture into deals without ever thinking of the outcome and never looked back.

George was a little more ornery than Peanutt, and George loved it when he could make someone squirm. If he thought he could get you into trouble, he'd get a kick out of it. Once, we were in Lakeland, Florida celebrating Peanutt's birthday. George wanted Peanutt to go to town with him. It was one of the few times I didn't accompany them, and they weren't away very long. Peanutt later told me what George did while they were gone.

"Charlene," he explained, "when George and I went to town the other day, George offered to pay for me a prostitute for my birthday. I told him that I didn't do stuff like that."

George just died laughing at him. Peanutt said he knew George was just picking at him and being ornery, but he felt like he needed to tell me.

"Peanutt, George wouldn't have known what to do if you'd taken him up on his offer. It would've scared him to death!"

George loved doing little things like that. If I had ever thought George was serious, he would have gotten his ears burnt by the chewing I would have unleashed on him. I never told George that I knew about his prank. George was a teaser and liked pulling pranks just to watch people squirm.

Bill and Nancy Giles lived next door to us, and we were well acquainted with them. They were always hearing about what went on around our house. One night, Peanutt sneaked away from home. He was drinking, and I wouldn't let him have any of the car keys, so he was on foot. We had four vehicles (two Cadillacs, a Vega Station Wagon, and a soft-top Jeep). I knew Peanutt would sneak back home and try to take one of the cars. I also thought he probably had a secret set of keys somewhere. I took a bobby pin, went outside, and let the air out of all sixteen tires. Bill Giles was in his yard and saw me.

"What in the world are you doing out here?" He yelled.

"I'm flattening the tires, so Peanutt can't take one of the cars," I yelled back to him.

Bill was dying laughing. He thought I was crazy. Later that night, Peanutt did come back and grabbed one of the cars. To my surprise, he took the Vega and drove across the neighbor's yard on four flats. He drove to the nearest service station and had the flats fixed. I knew he was headed to Nashville because earlier we had a heated argument about him going to Nashville. I called the Lawrenceburg Police and told them to stop him and put him in jail because he was drunk and shouldn't be driving. They said they would put out a bulletin to be on the lookout for Peanutt's Vega Station Wagon.

I called Sue Richards and told her to come and pick me up and not to take time to put on makeup. I called the police again and asked if they had seen Peanutt? They said they had stopped him, but he didn't seem drunk, so they let him go. I was furious. I told the cops I was going to be coming through Lawrenceburg, and I was going to be doing about 90 mph, and they had better not stop me. Sue and I headed to Nashville. We drove it in one hour and forty-five minutes. Just as we reached Franklin, Tennessee, Sue noticed Peanutt's car parked beside a phone booth. I slammed on the brakes and slid into the parking lot. Peanutt was on the phone with Nancy Giles asking her if she knew where I was? She told him that someone had come and picked me up. About that time, he saw me and was shocked that I had gotten to Franklin as fast as I had. I made him get into the car with me and ride home. Sue drove the Vega. I chewed his rear end out all the way home. I told him that there were twelve more flats for him to fix when he got home. He was furious, but I didn't care. I also told him that if he ever slipped away from me again, I was going to do something that would really make him mad. It was a long time before he tried sneaking off.

Later on, Peanutt told me about the police who stopped him in Lawrenceburg. He said they pulled him over and asked him where he was going, and he said to Nashville to see George Jones. He said there were three cars of policemen, and one wore a gold badge on his hat. The important cop asked if he was drunk, and he told him he had only had a couple of beers, and that he just wanted to get away from his wife for a little while.

"Go ahead and enjoy yourself," a cop jokingly commented. "I'd like to be going with you, but I have to work."

The cops told him that they would call Columbia, Tennessee and tell them to let him go on through. Peanutt came to Columbia, and a cop saw him and threw his hand up as Peanutt went by.

Bobby and Mary Womble were our friends. Back in that day, CB Radios were very popular, and the Wombles used theirs religiously. They were on there all the time.

Everybody liked Bobby. His CB name was "Cook," Peanutt's was "Mohair Sam," and mine was "Sweet Pea." They had gotten acquainted with George Jones and Linda (my sister). George's CB handle was "Possum" and Linda's was "Possum Queen". Linda and George were out of town when Bobby called and wanted Peanutt and me to go to Huntsville, Alabama to see Jerry Lee Lewis perform. I didn't want to go because I knew he would want to drink, and then Peanutt would drink.

There was another couple going, and I didn't like them, so I told Peanutt that we weren't going. Bobby called me and promised that nobody would drink a drop if I'd go. I finally gave in, but only under the condition that I would drive my own car, and they could ride with Peanutt and me.

We arrived in Huntsville and drove straight to the Carousel Club where Jerry Lee was going to perform. The house band was playing, so they all wanted to dance. When we got back to our table, Cook ordered a drink for everybody. I shocked them all when I said: "If you're buying everybody else a drink, just order me one too."

Peanutt had that deer in the headlights look on his face. He knew how much I hated alcohol.

"What do you want, Sweet Pea?" Cook asked tongue in cheek.

"I want a straight double shot of Vodka," I replied.

Peanutt chimed in, "Charlene, you can't handle that, that will wipe you out."

"I want what I asked for," I told him, and Cook ordered the drinks.

I planned this whole business out very carefully, so I knew what I was going to do. They had lied to me, and I wasn't about to stick around them. I was headed out the door and to my car, but I knew Peanutt was never going to let me drive off with that much alcohol in my system, so he would have to go with me.

The band was playing, and the woman I didn't like said to everybody:

"I'm gonna dance with Peanutt on the next song."

"Go ahead," I said, but I was thinking to myself, "*You do and you'll be sorry.*"

The next song started, and she took Peanutt's arm and started walking toward the dance floor. She laid her head on Peanutt's shoulder. It made me madder than the devil. While they were dancing, I got my keys out of my purse and went for the door. When I was almost to my car, I looked around, and they were all coming toward me waddling like ducks. I got in the car and put the keys in the ignition. Peanutt grabbed the door handle and opened the door.

"There's no way I'll let you drive this car home; you've had a drink," he said.

He took the keys from me and got in on the driver's side. The three men rode in the front seat and the three women in the back. The woman I was mad at was sitting next to the door. I kept thinking about her head lying on Peanutt's shoulder.

"I want you to know that I don't like you, I never have, and I never will. I want you to hear this from me personally, so you will know that it's not hearsay," I boldly told the woman.

"Sweet Pea," she curtly said, "You're insanely jealous."

I reached across the seat and slapped her in the face.

"Charlene, you stop that and stop it now!" Peanutt yelled.

I hauled off and slapped the fire out of him, too.

"You all lied to me, and now you're gonna pay for it," I yelled back.

"Sweet Pea, don't you say another word, or I'll slap you myself," Cook said.

Cook only had a few hairs on the top of his head, so I reached up and pulled out what hair he had.

Peanutt then decided to pull off the road and try to settle me down. I got out of the car.

"I want you to behave yourself," Peanutt said. "Now stop this mess and let's go home."

When we settled down, we got back in the car, but I was nowhere near finished. I told the gal that I hated her.

"I knew it would be like this, and that's why I didn't want to come up here tonight," I explained, and then I slapped the fire out of her again.

Peanutt pulled over to the side of the road again, and we emptied the car. He left the keys in the ignition, so I jumped in the car and drove off. Peanutt barely got in the car before I was gone. The others I left standing on the side of the road between Athens and Huntsville. I would not go back and get them. I didn't know how they'd get home, and I didn't care.

The next morning Cook was on the CB radio. He was telling everybody about what happened the night before. He broadcast that I had abandoned them on the side of the road, and that they had to ride home on the back of a flat bed truck all the way from Huntsville to Florence.

Peanutt was beyond mad at me. When we went to bed, he kept his clothes on, and I knew then that he was planning on leaving during the night. I tried my best to stay awake but being completely worn out, I fell asleep. The next morning, Peanutt was gone. He didn't come home all day or night. He didn't call or do anything to let me know he was all right. I thought to myself, "*I know what*

I'll do, I'll get him worried." I knew he would be listening to the CB radio in his car. I turned on the radio and then turned the volume up as high as it would go. I believed everybody in America listening to our channel would hear it. I keyed the microphone:

"This is Sweet Pea, and I want to sell everything that Mohair and I have. I want to start with the Browning CB radio and all the equipment that goes with it. I will sell the whole works for $1000.00. I know that's very cheap, but Mohair is gone, and I'm selling everything today, so I can be gone when he comes home. The first person that calls can have it."

About ten people answered all at once wanting to buy it. I had a man call me on the landline, and I told him that if Peanutt wasn't home by 5:00 p.m., he could come and pick it up. He said, "it's a deal."

"The CB radio has been sold," I broadcast next, "but I have a house full of expensive furniture, and I'm selling all of it too. I also have several guns for sale."

Several people again answered immediately and wanted to buy the guns and furniture. Each time, I'd have them call me on the phone, and I would tell them I'd have to wait and see if Peanutt came home or not. If he didn't, I'd sell all the items I promised. In about forty-five minutes, Peanutt had a friend of ours call me. He said that Peanutt was with him and wanted to know if he could come home.

"You tell Peanutt that it's up to him. He can come home if he wants but if he doesn't, it will be just fine." I said.

In about twenty minutes, they pulled in the driveway.

"What are you doing?" Peanutt asked. "I heard you were selling everything we have."

"Yes, and if you hadn't come home when you did, it would have all been gone by 5:00 p.m. including me."

"How in the world could you do such a thing?" he incredulously asked.

I was never invited by Cook to go anywhere else. That's exactly what I wanted. I was fed up with Peanutt drinking and sneaking away from me. I simply decided that each time he ran off,

I was going to take drastic measures, and I did. I had him put in jail for driving drunk so many times that they finally took his driver's license from him. For several weeks, he had to endure education classes for "Driving Under the Influence." I decided this was good for him and me because for a long time, I had to drive him everywhere he went. He sure was happy when they gave back his license and allowed him to drive again.

The District Attorney in Florence, Alabama was a good friend of ours. He was a jolly fellow and a lot of fun to be around. He always got a kick out of me for being the way I was.

One night Peanutt left the house walking. We had a disagreement over something, and he had been drinking. I thought he was probably somewhere in the neighborhood waiting for a chance to get one of our cars without me knowing it, so I decided to scare him. I went into the bedroom and got the pistol out of the nightstand drawer. I had never fired a gun in my life, but I was about to have my first experience at it. The gun was loaded with a full round in the chamber. I sat down on top of the bed and leaned back against the headboard. I fired the .45 Magnum Smith and Wesson pistol into the ceiling of our bedroom discharging six rounds. Each bullet left a hole in the ceiling about the size of a pencil eraser.

"Oh, well," I thought, *"That's not too bad. He can fix that easily."*

I waited about thirty minutes, and he didn't show up. The neighbors called the police, and they came to investigate the gunshots. I told the cops that Peanutt was drunk, had shot holes in the bedroom ceiling, then ran away on foot, and they needed to find him and put him in jail. They knew Peanutt. They turned on their spotlights and went up and down each street looking for him. They couldn't find him but said if I had any more trouble to give them a call. I got on the phone and called Lavern Tate. He was the District Attorney. Lavern lived close enough to our house that Peanutt could have gone there. I had called Lavern many times late at night, and it would take him forever to answer the phone. This time, he answered on the first ring.

"Lavern, have you seen Peanutt?" I asked.

"No Charlene, I haven't seen him. Why?"

"Peanutt took off again, and no one knows where he is. He probably found somebody to give him a lift to Nashville. I'm sorry, Laverne, for waking you up this late," I answered.

I hung up the phone. I knew Peanutt was at his house. I knew they thought I was going to just go to bed and give up for the night. They were wrong. I grabbed my purse, keys, and took off for Lavern's house. The lights were on. I went to the door and rang the bell. Lavern came to the door and opened it and when he did, I took my elbow and sank it into his big belly.

"Move over, I know you lied to me. I know Peanutt is here," I directed.

I made my way into the den, and Peanutt was lying on the couch. I told him to wake up and scoot over.

"I'm gonna sleep here with you." I demanded.

"What are you doing here?" He answered.

"Better yet, what are you doing here?" I asked him.

"You better get some rest Peanutt because there's work for you to do tomorrow. What kind of work?"

"I fired your pistol and shot six holes in our bedroom ceiling. They're only small holes."

"Charlene, do you realize that is a Magnum pistol? The bullets make bigger holes when they're exiting whatever they hit," he frantically explained.

"How can it make holes in the attic?" I asked.

"No, the roof! Do you realize we'll have to put a whole new roof on our house?"

"Peanutt, you know I don't care! If you had been home where you belong, none of this would have happened."

"Let's go to sleep; we'll worry about it tomorrow." Peanutt seemed casual about this because there was nothing he could do about it except get the roof fixed.

It sounds like I am a mean and controlling woman. I am

not like that at all. I was and am a woman who loves my husband, and I knew he was a better person than that. I wanted Peanutt to stop his drinking because drinking and getting drunk lead Peanutt to nothing but trouble, but with everything I tried in our marriage, nothing made him give up his desire for alcohol.

One great day, Peanutt met a man who had more power and influence over him than I did. Only a very powerful man could get that much attention from Peanutt. When Peanutt came to know the Lord Jesus Christ as his personal Savior, he stopped drinking and quit all his other bad habits such as smoking. The Lord changed his whole life. He became a new man; he became a Christian, and he never went back to his old ways of living.

Peanutt is today the man I always knew he could be, and our lives are so much better now. We've been really blessed and thank God for it all. Bill and Nancy Giles come by our business every now and then, and we can look back on all that happened and have a good laugh. Nancy says she doesn't know how in the world we stayed together all those years. She explains that Bill will never forget the sound of that air coming out of all those tires I deflated. I'm just thankful it all changed, and we are living a peaceful, happy life. That's all I ever wanted or ever dreamed would happen.

....

CHAPTER TEN

Virginia Wynette Pugh - Wife Number Three

Virginia Wynette Pugh (Tammy Wynette) was born on May 5,1942 in Itawamba County, Mississippi, in the small town of Tremont. She was the only child of Hollis and Mildred Pugh. Her father died of a brain tumor before Tammy turned one year old. Tammy was too young to remember him, but she was told he was a very talented musician. She would sit on his lap at the piano, and he would stretch her fingers over the piano keys. She believed that was the reason she loved the piano so much.

Tammy's mother was a schoolteacher and when Tammy was four years old, her mother married Foy Lee. Foy and Mildred moved to Memphis, Tennessee and because Tammy's grandparents wanted to raise her, her mother allowed it, and Tammy grew up living in her grandparent's home. Tammy always gave her dad the credit for her musical talents. She taught herself to play by ear on an old piano in her school's gym.

Folks around Tremont would gather at the Providence Church near where Tammy lived to hear her play the piano and sing. It has been said that when Tammy would sing, it would raise the hair on people's arms and send chills down their spines.

Tammy loved her grandparents and spoke highly of all the folks she was raised with around Tremont. She talked a lot about her Aunt Carolyn, who was no doubt special to Tammy. She also talked about her playmates, her friends, and school classmates. I can't recall all their names, but I especially remember her talking about Agnes and Thad Wilson. In fact, Tammy kept close contact with Agnes her entire life. Tammy grew up with the responsibility of working around the house and in the fields. Even though it's been said that her grandparents spoiled Tammy, they made sure a work ethic was instilled in her. Like most all the other children growing up in that part of the country, she helped take care of the farm animals and worked in the cotton fields.

Tammy loved to tell stories about her childhood days. She'd always laugh and giggle as she reminisced about how hard those times were. She once said that as a young girl, she thought that having country ham, cathead biscuits, and gravy for breakfast was a sign of being poor but when she got older, she realized it was some pretty good grub.

Tammy was proud of her roots and loved to go back there to visit every chance she got. On one visit to Tremont, she went to a field where she once worked and made a bouquet out of cotton stalks, complete with snow-white cotton in the bows. She took the bouquet back to her mansion on Franklin Road in Nashville, placed it in a very expensive and elegant vase, and displayed it in the living room. It became a real conversation piece and gave Tammy a good reason to tell some of her cotton-picking stories. She once said:

"You can bet your rear-end you'll learn things from living in the country on a farm that you would never learn in a school book."

As she became older, Tammy grew tired of the cotton fields, the animals, and all the chores that farm life called for. It had gotten rather boring working the fields and being guarded by her grandparents. Her interests had changed. She loved to sing and play the piano, and that became her primary interest. It was time to pave some new avenues for her to take in life. Down one of these new roads, she met a young man by the name of Euple Byrd. She started dating Euple even though she had a lot of young fellows interested in her. Tammy had already gotten pretty popular around her part of the country from playing and singing anywhere and anytime she got a chance. She'd sing at various schools, churches, and a number of other places around the country. If there was an opportunity, she took it. She finally married Euple Byrd. He was a few years older than Tammy and had just gotten out of the Marines. They married in 1959. The new Mrs. Byrd thought for the first time in her life she had the freedom to do whatever she pleased. It was a little disappointing when it didn't turn out that way.

The first big surprise came when she found out she was pregnant with their first child. She gave birth to Gwendolyn Lee Byrd on April 15, 1961. It didn't stop there. On August 2, 1962, she gave birth to her second daughter, Jacquelyn Fay Byrd. Tammy had her hands full. Times by now were getting rough on the young Byrd family. Euple was having a hard time finding work to do. It was hard to make enough to just feed the family, let alone living expenses. They lived in an old shack of a house with weather beaten boards on it. There was no paint on it at all. It was up a dirt road and had no heat or air, just an old fireplace. Tammy took me to that house one day. As we rode up the old, washed out road, straddling gullies in her Eldorado, she said,

"I have lots of memories of this place you're about to see," She said. "You know, just seeing this house gives me the shivers, I thought I'd freeze to death in that house."

At the young age of twenty-one, with two baby daughters already on her lap, Tammy found out she was pregnant again. Euple couldn't support the four of them let alone five. Tammy knew that she was going to have to do something and do it in a hurry. She started cosmetology school and got her license. Her marriage to Euple was beginning to crumble. Tammy decided that she and her girls were going to move to Birmingham, Alabama and live with the other grandparents. That's exactly what she did and went to work in a beauty salon once she got there. Tammy got an opportunity to audition for "The Country Boy Eddie Show." It was a well-known TV program, and Tammy was accepted on the show. She loved it, and it encouraged her to push her talents further into the limelight. She'd do shows in various places with Country Boy Eddie. This really gave her the fever to try for the big time, but she'd wait until after the third child was born. Tina Denise Byrd was born in 1965.

Tammy finally quit her beautician job and The Country Boy Eddie Show and set out for Nashville in 1966 with her three girls. She was highly discouraged by her family members and friends, but nothing was going to stop her from busting Nashville wide open. She was Nashville bound and bound to stay when she got there come hell or high water, and that's exactly what she did. After going from one record label to another and all of them turning her down, she began to get a little worried. She desperately needed someone to believe in her as much as she believed in herself. Peanutt and I were in the room at the Biltmore Motel when she came in to meet with Pappy Daily. Pappy was George Jones' producer and owned Musicor Record Label, which George was signed to. Tammy auditioned for Pappy, but Pappy turned her down, too.

We were in Nashville to pick up some songs for George to record the next day. Tammy came to George's session at Columbia Studio B. She sat over in the corner with Peanutt and me, and some of the other writers who were there for George's session. She was cute as a bug in a rug with her hair pulled up in a donut on top of her head. She smiled all the time. I found out later that Tammy had always idolized George. Tammy kept knocking on doors until one day she finally knocked on the right one. A door that would take her straight to the top of country music. She not only kept her determination to get signed to a label, but she also had a responsibility to feed, clothe, and provide for three little girls. Time and money were running out from all sources, and she was desperate by now. Tammy finally found what she had been looking for at the CBS building where she met Billy Sherrill. Billy Sherrill really liked her voice and liked Tammy as well. It just so happened that Billy was looking for a female artist to produce, and the timing for Tammy was perfect. It was Billy who gave her the name, Tammy Wynette.

Billy signed her to Epic Records and started looking for songs. He wanted the perfect songs. He found that song when he heard, *"Apartment Number 9."* They cut it and released it as a single. It was Tammy's first hit record and stayed on the charts for nine weeks. Her next release was, *"Your Good Girl's Gonna Go Bad."* It soared to the top of the charts like a rocket. It went to number three on the country charts. The ball was now rolling for Tammy. Just about every record Billy released with her was a hit. He released six more hits, one after the other, all going to number one on the national charts. They were: *"I Don't Wanna Play House,"* *"Take Me to Your World,"* *"D-i-v-o-r-c-e,"* *"Stand by Your Man,"* *"Singing My Song,"* and *"The Way to Love a Man."* Her biggest hit ever was *"Stand by Your Man."* Tammy's determination paid off. The family members and friends back in Tremont could not believe that Virginia Wynette Pugh, now known as Tammy Wynette, had hit the big time.

Agnes Wilson had been a close friend to Tammy from their grammar school years. Tammy had gotten so busy, and she realized she had to have some help. Who but Agnes could Tammy count on? Agnes became Tammy's right arm. She and her husband, "Thad," were immediately added to Tammy's family of friends. Agnes had always told Tammy that she'd be a star someday. Agnes could not have been more right. Tammy looked at Agnes for all kinds of help with the kids, the house, or anything else Tammy needed. She totally trusted Agnes and Thad. Sometimes, they would embarrass the kids (on purpose) by picking them up from school in the limo. They practically had to live with Tammy to help her out.

Peanutt and I were around George all the time. We were in Nashville with George one day, and we knew there was something different going on. He was overly chipper and in such an unusually good mood. There was some whispering going on, so we knew whatever he was up to had to be kept quiet. George was animated like he had ants in his pants; he could not be still. He was anxious and fidgety. After a while, we overheard George say to his manager, "I love her already." We knew then that it all had to do with some woman, but we didn't know who. George was still married to Shirley at the time, so we were surprised at his remark. Of course, we also knew that his and Shirley's marriage was really shaky and had been a while. We never dreamed that the woman he was speaking of was Tammy Wynette. She was married to Don Chapel. I'm sure that's why George was trying to keep everything hush-hush until they could get out of their situations. George and Tammy were having an affair but had to keep it hid until they got a divorce.

George divorced Shirley in 1968, but Tammy was still married to Don. Don had not been good to Tammy or the children. George knew about it and got very upset with Don but couldn't say anything to him because she was Don's wife. George was drinking one particular day and decided he wanted to go visit Tammy at her house. After all, he had cut one of Don's songs and should have a right to drop by and see them. George knew that Don was irritable with the kids. He knew Don would get mad at Tammy and call her names. He also knew Tammy was fed up with Don's bossy spirit and was ready to get out of the marriage. George was in love with Tammy and had waited as long as he was going to wait. He was tired of the slipping around thing.

During George's visit with Don and Tammy that day, Don was ranting and raving on Tammy and the kids. They all got upset and were crying. Tammy got onto Don for fussing at the kids, so Don started cursing her and calling her names. George could not take it any longer, so he came to Tammy's defense. He didn't care if he was in another man's house. His love for Tammy outweighed the thought of the trouble he could get into. Don warned George to stay out of his business and asked George why was it any of his business how he treated Tammy. George boldly answered by saying,

"It's a lot of my business, I love her. I love Tammy." George and Tammy had been seeing each other prior to that day but had not actually had an intimate affair. They were aware that they loved each other. During George and Don's heated argument, George blurted out to Don,

"Tammy loves me too, don't you Tammy?" George turned to Tammy to confirm his remark and she answered,

"Yes, I do."

At this point they both realized it was time to get out of there. She grabbed the kids, George kicked over the table, and George, Tammy, and the three girls left the premises together. They were the talk all over Nashville.

Once George and Tammy were together, they were as happy as they could be. Neither one of them cared what anybody thought about their relationship. They no longer hid their love from anybody because they knew that they would soon get married. George had accepted Tammy's three girls as if they were his own. Their only problem was that Tammy was not yet divorced from Don. They had to figure out how to get that divorce quickly, so they could get married. Don was furious, and Tammy thought he might give her a hard time about giving her a divorce. Somehow, Tammy found out that her marriage to Don was not legal, and she didn't have to file and then wait for a divorce to be final. Tammy and George took off to Ringo, Georgia and got married in a little wedding chapel. It was like they had found heaven right here on earth.

....

CHAPTER ELEVEN

George and Tammy - Two Legends Under One Roof

Major changes were brewing for George and Tammy. George left Musicor Records and signed with Epic Records. He wanted to team up with Tammy and release duets. Wow! What a team! Billy Sherrill was reputed to be the best producer in Nashville, and they were blessed to have him. The parting from Musicor was an expensive move for George. He had to give up a portion of his royalties to the label in order to get out of his contract. He had divorced Shirley and had to give up a portion of his royalties to her as part of the settlement. Shirley never asked for the royalties for herself; she wanted the royalties to support their sons, Jeffrey and Brian, so they would have income for the rest of their lives. I supported Shirley because I knew the boys well. They were sweet kids, and the boys deserved every dime.

The impact of this arrangement meant that George's living resources had to be made through his concerts and future royalties. George was hot in 1969 and 1970 but by 1972, his career was slipping downhill. He recorded a hit song, *"Right Won't Touch a Hand,"* that made it to the top ten, but he desperately needed a number one record. When he left Musicor and signed with Epic, he was ready for a change and needed a change. Tammy was already on Epic, and Billy Sherrill was already her producer.

It was very hard for George to leave Pappy Daily because he had been under Pappy's wings for such a long time. Pappy had been by George's side for so long that he actually treated him like a son.

It hurt Pappy when George left him, but Pappy also realized George needed a change and didn't hold it against him.

Billy Sherrill was the hottest producer in Nashville, and George could not have made a better, more positive move. George's releases would receive the marketing and promotion he had always needed but didn't have. George was a little nervous about being on the new label and not knowing Billy Sherrill very well. Even though neither George nor Billy knew what to expect from each other, once they got into the studio, they did fine together. Billy wasted no time letting George know that he had new ideas for George's sessions. Things were going to change from what George was used to, and George never argued; he let Billy have his way about things, and he realized that Billy took as much great pride in what he produced as George would. He worked on a session until he thought it was a masterpiece and most of the time, it was. George realized he was fortunate to have Billy as his producer. George wanted and needed a hit record, and Billy was only interested in producing hits.

Billy was good at letting George pick some of his own material. If George liked a song, he could sing it better. If he didn't like a certain song, it became a chore for him to sing it. Billy changed George's style by lowering his voice a couple of keys, and that resulted in making his voice into a more pleasant tone. He added strings and different instruments to George's sessions that made his music fuller and more up to date. George wasn't comfortable with the new sound at first but as he and Billy worked together, George realized Billy knew what he was doing, and George trusted Billy's judgment. "*We Can Make It*" was George's first release with Epic in 1972. It soared to number six on the charts. The next release was, "*Loving You Could Never Be Better.*" This is the song that Peanutt and I co-wrote, but he would not play it for George and Tammy because he didn't think it was good enough, and he didn't want to waste their time.

Because I am half a writer, I insisted several times that night at George and Tammy's house that Peanutt pitch the song that I had written for them.

"Peanutt, I want to hear the song Charlene's trying to get you to pitch," Tammy said.

Peanutt played the song, and Tammy loved it. She told Peanutt to go to the studio and put the song down and get a tape back to them as soon as he could. George was to record the very next day. Peanutt went to a studio, recorded the song, and brought the tape to George and Tammy.

"George is doing that song," Tammy said.

We went straight to the studio, and George recorded it. *Loving You Could Never Be Better* became his next single and went all the way to number two on the national charts. I won my first BMI award for that song.

This release was the beginning of George's new classic country sound, and it was definitely a plus for George. In 1972, George and Tammy engaged in recording duet records. They cut a couple duet songs, *"Ceremony"* and *"Old Fashioned Singing."* Later on, they recorded *"Let's Build a World Together."* They had beautiful harmony in their singing, but the harmony in their marriage was getting a little off key. They were having some trouble getting along. They finally split up for a short while and then got back together.

Peanutt and I were on the road full time with George and Tammy at this time, and one day the two of them were nagging at each other. Peanutt heard George say:

"We've got to hold on, Tammy."

What George said stuck in Peanutt's head. That night, we got back to the motel and checked in. George had been drinking a little and so had Peanutt. Tammy was pretty irritated at both of them and didn't mind letting Peanutt know that she was hacked at them. Once we got checked into our room, Peanutt thought he needed to do something to get Tammy back into his good graces. He decided to go down to the lounge. He had just enough alcohol in his system to make him ornery. He took a seat at the bar and started thinking about Tammy getting on him, so he decided to retaliate. He ordered a round of drinks for all the other folks sitting in the bar and had the bill put on Tammy's tab. It was over three hundred dollars. He wasn't worried at the moment about what he'd done because he was getting back at her. It was when he got back to the room and reality hit him that he got worried about it.

"I've got to do something to keep Tammy from getting all over me," Peanutt said to me.

I told him that he did it, so he would have to fix it. I was really aggravated with him; not only for what he did, but because he was drinking. Tammy didn't want him drinking; especially, when he and George were together.

Peanutt came up with a great idea of how to make amends to Tammy and keep her from chewing out his rear end. He picked up his guitar and started singing, *"We're Gonna Hold On."* He had thought of what George said to Tammy that day on the bus and wrote the song. Peanutt couldn't wait to let George and Tammy hear it.

The first thing the next morning, Peanutt took his guitar to their room. We sat on the side of the bed.

"Tammy," Peanutt said, "I've got a song going that will be a great duet for you and George. I want to play it for you."

Peanutt began to sing, and George had a fit over it. George and Peanutt couldn't wait, so they finished it before Peanutt and me had left the room. Peanutt knew he and George had written another good song, and he also knew he was off the hook with Tammy.

We were all on the bus leaving Jamestown, Pennsylvania, and Tammy came up to the front wearing a half-cocked smile:

"Peanutt, did you have a good time last night?"

Peanutt grinned at her and said,

"Yeah Tammy, I did, but I'm sorry for what I did to you."

"That's okay Peanutt," Tammy replied, "but don't you ever do that again." Peanutt was ashamed of what he did, but nothing else was said about it.

Later on, it became one of Tammy's favorite stories to tell, and she'd laugh about it as she'd tell it.

In 1973, George and Tammy recorded Peanutt's song, *"We're Gonna Hold On."* It was their first number one duet. The lyrics spelled out the truth about them. Their marriage was shaky, but both were desperately trying to make it work. The song was perfect for them, and the fans knew it. It said exactly what the fans wanted to hear. They had been hearing about the split and all that stuff, so it gave them hope that George and Tammy would make it. People who loved George and Tammy were concerned about them. They were one of America's favorite soap operas, and people wanted to know every detail of their lives because George and Tammy were an all American dream couple together. They had everything going for them, but they were together all the time. They were on the road together, at home together, recording together, and I think both needed some room to breathe.

Tammy didn't trust George because of his drinking. She was afraid to be away from him because she knew he'd mess up. She had to think about whether he'd be out and not come back in time to leave for their next concert dates. It posed a big problem for her. She worried all the time about their relationship. She tried as hard as she could to keep the marriage functioning.

I think that George loved Tammy, but he wanted to stretch his wings. In order to do that, he'd find excuses to get away from the house. He'd tell Tammy he was going to the barbershop and once he was gone, he stayed gone. He wouldn't come home sometimes for a couple of days. Tammy would be furious. She'd pack up the kids and take them out to the farm at Spring Hill where her mother and stepfather lived. Sometimes she'd stay there until George called. Then again, sometimes she'd hide out from him for a day or two. When he did return home, she wouldn't be there and he'd call around but couldn't find her. It became like a cat chasing a mouse. The situation became worse when George would not show up for performances. Tammy and the band would take off and leave George behind. Tammy would do the performances by herself and try to explain why George was not there. She'd make excuses for him. It got to the point where she didn't know what to expect. Sometimes George would fly to the dates and show up just in time for the concert. The marriage was becoming more and more stormy, and nobody knew what would happen next.

In the beginning of the marriage, they were both so happy. Tammy was exactly what George needed, and George was exactly what Tammy needed. George thought Tammy could do anything. She was a good singer, she could write hit songs, she could harmonize, she was an extremely good cook, and she was a good mother. She had given him a daughter, Georgette. He thought, *"What My Woman Can't Do, Can't be Done."*

Tammy had the same feelings about George. He knew how to decorate a home better than a woman could. He was a legend. He could sing, write, and pick a guitar. He was good to her girls. He was the perfect man, but they became restless. Tammy was always looking at homes. She'd take George to see this house and that house, and they never stayed at one place very long before they would move on. It seemed that when they encountered problems, they'd run off and leave them all behind.

Tammy knew George liked to decorate. She felt that it would be exciting for George if they would move, and it would give him something to do that he really enjoyed. A change would keep them both busy and would provide a new atmosphere. Tammy also knew that George got tired of the same old walls. He liked changes; especially, in his everyday life. George had to stay busy. Tammy wanted to keep him involved with things that kept him at home. That worked, but only until the job was done. Tammy ran out of schemes to keep George busy. Tammy also became tired of the effort she was putting forth to make things work for them. She finally developed an attitude. She kept thinking,

"Who the devil does he think he is? Why do I have to chase after this man, why ain't he chasing after me?"

She thought she had as much to offer as he did. She was right about that. I had much sympathy for Tammy, and I had equal sympathy for George. They had everything anyone would ever dream about: beautiful homes, cars, fancy buses, expensive clothes, fine jewelry, lake homes, farm houses, hit records, good children, and plenty of money. They had everything you could want but happiness. America's Country Music dream couple became miserable.

Tammy's emotions finally got her to the point that she had to take a stand against George. She'd do little things that she knew would upset him. I think this started happening once she had made her mind up that she wasn't going to put up with him. She came to a point where it really didn't matter anymore. She was tired. She was also having some stomach trouble and was in and out of the hospital a lot. She became dependent on pain pills. The pills did not help her when she had her mood swings, and she'd do something that would irritate George off to the core. She felt it was her turn to nag and pick at him, and she did. There were a couple of lady friends that were always supporting Tammy by putting George down. They were close to Tammy, were also employed by Tammy, and were right up Tammy's nose in everything she did.

I never thought George and Tammy would actually get a divorce. I thought they'd fuss and feud but would work it out before they would actually file. I think their desire to be independent plus the fact they were both spoiled by the luxuries afforded by their careers would eventually be their undoing.

George and Tammy first lived in George's house after they married. They then moved to Tammy's house because it had more room. Next, they moved to Lakeland, Florida to the house George received in the divorce settlement from his first wife, Shirley. They left that house and moved to an antebellum home on 40 acres just outside of Lakeland. It was on this property that they built the Old Plantation Music Park. George loved that park. He worked continuously on the project ensuring that it would be ready to open for regular concerts. He wanted to settle down there and do his own thing. He wanted to curtail his performances, get off the road, and promote the music park.

George was approaching forty years old. He had worked the road since he was a teenager, so he was ready to stay home for a while. Tammy was pregnant with Georgette and was expecting her to be born any day. George had just about quit drinking entirely and had thrown his heart and soul into the park. He did everything he could think of to make it successful. He had a mobile home park with electric hookups and a playground for the kids. He even provided transportation to help the handicapped and elderly to get to the show area. They had golf carts, a swimming pool, and the house had been brought up to date and was absolutely beautiful.

George had an unbelievable rule, *"No alcoholic beverages allowed on the grounds of the plantation."* George and Tammy had it all. They had food stands and picnic tables and by the time it was time for the opening show, George had everything in tip-top shape.

The first show was a major success. There was space provided for eleven thousand people, and it was packed to capacity. Every event was a huge success, and George was so preoccupied that he seldom drank. He loved what he was doing, but Tammy became lethargic and bored, and that led to her becoming extremely restless.

George expanded the park and added an antique car museum that contained all sorts of expensive antique cars. George was very proud of the work he had done and achieving what he had set out to accomplish.

George called Peanutt and me. He wanted us to come down to Florida and spend a week with Tammy and him. He wanted us to bring True to play with Tina, Tammy's daughter. My first look at the park took my breath away it was so beautiful, and much more than I ever expected.

George and Tammy took us on a VIP tour of the park. They introduced us to their best friends in Florida, Cliff and Maxine Hyder. We spent the week with George and Tammy as they'd asked us to do. We had a wonderful time. Peanutt and I were so proud of them, and what they had accomplished. Tammy and I had plenty of time to talk while George and Peanutt spent time roaming the forty acres and admiring the antique cars. Tammy confided in me that she loved that place and was so thankful George had quit drinking. She was thankful he was so happy, but she was bored stiff there. Tammy wanted to go back to Nashville.

"I know it would take an act of God to get George away from this place," she commented.

About the fourth night we were there, I got the fire scared out of me. George and Tammy had already gone to bed. Peanutt and I were watching TV in our bedroom, and the kids had been asleep for a long time. All of a sudden, George and Tammy's dogs were having a fit. The peacocks were all acting up and making all kinds of strange sounds. I got up and went to George and Tammy's bedroom. I woke them up and told them something was going on outside.

"No Charlene, they all do that sometimes, it's okay. There's nothing wrong," Tammy explained.

I went back to our bedroom, but the peacocks and the dogs had not settled down. Tammy finally did get up and agreed that something did not sound right. George and Tammy met Peanutt and me in the hall. We all went outside together to check things out. Just as everybody got outside, Tammy turned around to close the door. It was then she noticed something written on the back of the door. "Pig" had been written in big, bold letters with red lipstick. We had just finished reading the Charles Manson story, and both of us were terrified.

All of us went back in the house. George called several friends and had them come over and Tammy called the Sheriff's office and had them come out. They all ganged up together with George and Peanutt and started searching all over the 40 acres to see if they could find anybody. I realized that Tammy and I were there in the house with no one to help us if someone tried to harm us.

"Tammy, we don't have anybody here with us," I said.

"Oh, my God," she said, "I never even thought about that. Let's go and lock ourselves in my bedroom!"

We locked ourselves in Tammy's bedroom, but that didn't

give us much comfort from the fright we were experiencing. We had been in there about ten minutes when we heard a loud noise. I began to tremble. Tammy panicked.

"What was that?" I screamed.

"I don't know," Tammy replied.

We crawled under her bed but soon Tammy calmed down.

"Charlene, I think I know what the noise was. I think it was the ice maker dumping a load of ice."

"Are you sure?"

"Yes, I'm almost sure that's what it was."

We crawled out from under the bed and continued to wait on the men to come back. It seemed like they had been gone forever. I was a nervous wreck.

George and Peanutt finally came up to the room.

"Well, we've looked the whole place over and didn't see a thing or a sign of anybody being here," George explained.

All the other people left, but I didn't sleep a wink all night long. I was ready to go home the next day, but George and Tammy insisted that we stay. We stayed the rest of the week, but I wanted to get away from there. I never knew who wrote on that door, and I'll never forget that night.

After we came home, we'd talk often to George and Tammy. There had been some more strange things happening around the park. I pondered about how Tammy had expressed her desire to move back to Nashville, and how she talked about being bored to tears while George was occupied with his own happiness. I became suspicious of Tammy. I wondered if somehow she was concocting the things in an attempt to scare George away from the park.

Time went on, and George began to get restless. He began drinking again. He began to get a little rough. Maybe it was because he knew Tammy was unhappy, and he felt like he was going to have to either give up his dream place or lose his wife. I'm not sure who thought what, or who did what. I just know that things had changed, and they were having big problems between them.

Tammy finally won the battle, and they moved back to Hendersonville, Tennessee. They moved to Tammy's beautiful house on Old Hickory Lake. Shortly after getting settled in Hendersonville, Tammy insisted that Peanutt and I move to Nashville. She had found a house that she thought we'd like. We went to Nashville and spent a few days with them. We spent time looking at houses. We settled on a house in Hendersonville on Walton Ferry Road.

Peanutt and I spent a lot of time with George and Tammy. We were always going into Nashville to see Billy Sherrill or to take care of business. On the way to Nashville one day, Tammy said,

"Peanutt, George and I are going to be gone this week and while we are out of town, I'd like for you and Charlene to look around for some land with a big house on it."

While they were gone, Peanutt and I found the perfect place. We couldn't wait to tell them about it. It was at Spring Hill, Tennessee just south of Nashville. It was a beautiful antebellum house sitting on three hundred forty acres of land. The price was very reasonable considering what was included with the package. We took them to see it as soon as they got home. They fell in love with it. They bought it and started making plans. They redecorated the house and had it all painted and hired different contractors to make any repairs it needed. George had people out there mending the fences and trimming up around the place. Tammy couldn't find curtains long enough for the windows and couldn't wait to have them made, so she bought king-sized sheets and made her own curtains for that entire house. They turned out beautiful.

Eventually, George and Tammy got restless again and decided the farm was too far from Hendersonville, so they started looking for a house in Nashville. It didn't take long to find one on Hillsboro Road. A few days later, they spotted another one they absolutely fell in love with, and so they bought it. The house was located on the top of a mountain on Tyne Boulevard in Nashville. Tammy called me,

"Charlene, George and I have found the perfect house for you and Peanutt, it's absolutely beautiful. It sits on four acres of prime property. We want you to see it."

Peanutt and I went to see the house, and we fell in love with it. Some of the property's main features were a large swimming pool, a brick fence all the way around the property, a big sunroom, and an open stairway that spanned the entire foyer. It was beautiful.

"Tammy, I'm not sure we can afford this house," I lamented.

"Oh, yes you can," she replied, "I'll cut some of Peanutt's songs and make sure you can make the payments."

Tammy told me that George and she had already put up earnest money on the house, but they changed their minds when they found the house on Tyne Boulevard.

"Okay," I explained, "but you'll have to wait until our house sells before we can pay you that earnest money back."

That was fine with Tammy, so we bought the house and put ours up for sale. Our house sold really quickly. We moved into our new home and put our daughter in school at Franklin Road Academy along with Tammy's girls, Tina, Gwen, and Jackie. Things were going great for us.

George, Tammy, Peanutt, and I were together all the time. We were writing one song after the other. George and Tammy were cutting hit records. Tammy's mother and stepfather, Mildred and Foy, were living at Spring Hill and taking care of the farm.

George and Tammy had spun out of control. They were shifting from place to place in an attempt to keep some excitement in their marriage, but it was coming to a halt. It was obvious they were wrestling with issues each one of them had. Peanutt and I would go over to their house a lot of times just to keep them occupied. We'd play Aggravation or Rook with them. We would suggest going on a cruise, or do whatever it took to keep George and Tammy on speaking terms. George wanted Peanutt and me to be at their house every morning by 8:00 a.m. He demanded it. We'd be there because we really didn't have anything else to do. We were signed to Tammy's publishing company, so we could write with George and Tammy if we felt like writing, and that's what we did most of the time.

One day, George had a recording session booked for Tammy and him to cut a duet album. There were about four other writers signed to Tammy's publishing company, Altam Records. They had been writing some songs, too. George Richey, Narrow Wilson, and Carmel Taylor had written a song that George and Tammy cut that day. Each of them owned one-third of the writer's rights on the one song. George and Tammy cut six of Peanutt's songs on that one album. Peanutt and I could feel the resentment from some of the other writers, and a jealousy developed that we were aware of but kept quiet about it.

I knew sooner or later it would all come out. It wasn't long until Tammy began to change towards Peanutt and me. We could feel the change because she wasn't treating us the same as she did before this happened. George knew it too, and he didn't like it at all.

George would get drunk, and Tammy would call Peanutt and me and tell us to go find him and if we found him, we were to keep him with us. One night, we were out looking for George. We found him and persuaded him to go home with us. We decided to take him to Florence, Alabama with us, so that he would not try and get away. After calling Tammy, we told her we had George with us, and that he was okay and not to worry because we'd take care of him.

While we were in Alabama, the alternator went out on our Cadillac. We had to get it fixed, and it took three days before we could get back to Nashville. During this time, we were never out of touch with Tammy. When we did get George back to Tammy, she was furious. She accused me of staying three days at the Tyne Boulevard house with George while Peanutt went to Alabama. She said that I had cooked for George and left rotten food all over the kitchen, and that there were seventeen empty whiskey bottles strewn around the house. I told her she was crazy, and that I had done no such thing, and George and Peanutt would verify I was with them the entire time.

"Somebody has started this mess to make you jealous of me. This is a conspiracy, Tammy, to break up our friendship. They are trying to destroy our relationship so that George and you won't record any more of Peanutt's songs. They are jealous and are trying to find a way to stop us from writing and if we don't put a stop to them, they will succeed."

Tammy continued talking to me, calling me, and making threats.

"I'll never cut another Peanutt Montgomery song," She said to me.

"That will be fine, Tammy. We will survive anyway," I replied.

She also said she would not allow her daughters to speak to my daughter. True absolutely loved those girls. She stayed with them when we were on the road and had been with them the whole time we were in Nashville. When this happened, True came home from school crying.

"Mama, I don't know what I've done but Jackie, Gwen, and Tina won't have anything to do with me. They wouldn't even speak to me today," True cried.

I knew what had happened. I told True that Tammy was mad at me, and that she had told the girls not to associate with her.

I'd had enough. I was not going to let my little girl be hurt by all this mess, so I called the real estate office and had them come over and put my house up for sale. I told them to bring a big sign because I wanted it to sell fast. A Realtor came and listed the house for sale. A few days later, Tammy saw the sign. She called.

"Charlene, why are you selling your house?" She asked.

"We are going to move back to Florence; we're going home." I replied.

"Oh, no, you can't sell your house, you love that place," She answered.

"Yes, I do, but I don't have to put up with this mess that's been going on, and I'm not going to let all this crap involve my daughter," I fired back at her. "She can't help how much George drinks, and she can't help what we do or you do, so she's not going to be hurt just because somebody is mad at us. Yes, we're going home."

Tammy tried to get me to change my mind but to no avail. The next weekend, Peanutt and I went to Florence and met with a builder, Bennett Wright. He had a new house already finished, but I didn't like it. We decided to let him custom build a house for us while ours was selling. Our Nashville house sold in two weeks. By the time our Nashville home closed escrow, Bennett had our new house built and ready for us to move. We were back home in Florence.

A short time later, George and Tammy purchased a huge house on Franklin Road in Nashville. This was truly a big house with seventeen thousand six hundred square feet of living area, sixteen bedrooms, and fifteen bathrooms.

We had not been with George and Tammy for a while. Peanutt and I tended to our own business in Florence and were getting settled into our new home on Milford Street in Sherwood Forest. Out of the clear blue, George called one day and wanted us to come to Nashville to see his new home. We were reluctant to go because we had not talked to Tammy and didn't know how she'd feel about it. George assured us that Tammy wanted us to come, and that we were welcome.

The Franklin Road house was beautiful. Tammy was very nice to us and so friendly it was as if nothing had ever happened.

When we started to leave, George followed us to the car.

"What street do you live on?" George asked.

"Milford Street," Peanutt replied.

"What's the house number?" George asked.

"2713."

"I'll see you later, Peanutt," George said while walking back toward the house.

Peanutt suspected George must be up to something.

"Well, I hope he doesn't do anything that would make Tammy mad at us again, but I bet he's planning on coming to Florence," I commented.

About three days later there was a knock at our door. I opened the door, and it was George. I was surprised.

"I told you that nobody could keep me away from you two, so here I am," George announced.

We were happy to see him, and he was proud to be there, but I had a feeling that he had sneaked away from Tammy, and I believed the phone would be ringing soon. Sure enough, about two hours later the phone rang. I went to the bedroom to answer because I felt for sure it was Tammy, and I knew I was not going to lie to her. I didn't want to squeal on George, and he had already told me that if Tammy called not to tell her he was with us. When she asked me if we had seen George, I told her yes, and that he was with us. I told her that he asked me not to tell her he was there. She asked if he was drunk, and I told her no, but that he had been drinking.

"Don't let him get away from you. Keep him with you and Peanutt," She said.

I promised her we would do our best to keep him with us, and I'd let her know if he should leave.

We talked every day, and I let her know every move George made. I felt sorry for her because I knew what it was like to be worried about a drunken husband. I was completely honest with Tammy. I really loved her; even though, she hurt me before we moved back to Florence. I had forgiven her, and I didn't hold anything against Tammy because I knew she loved George and wanted the marriage to work, but I felt it was impossible. I didn't blame her entirely for what she had accused me. I knew someone had tried to convince her that I was having an affair with George. She knew better, and we both knew that. She knew me well enough to know that I would not have let Peanutt come to Alabama without me. She knew how I felt about Peanutt, and that I wouldn't think about being unfaithful to him. George knew that too.

As it turned out, George continued coming to Alabama to see us. I was looking out a window in my house one afternoon, and a taxicab pulled into the driveway. George had hired a cab to drive him from Nashville to our house in Florence. Of course, he was drinking. He said he didn't have any keys to any of his cars, so he called a cab to take him to buy a car. The car broke down just outside of Nashville, so he called another cab to bring him to our house. The next morning, we drove George to Nashville to find the car. He had no idea what kind of car he had bought until we finally discovered it was a burgundy Oldsmobile.

In 1973, George recorded, *"Once You've Had the Best,"* and in 1974, *"The Door,"* and both songs were big hits produced by Billy Sherrill, and then George and Tammy's marriage was at the end. Everybody knew this was happening, but nobody wanted to accept it.

Some of our best years were with George and Tammy, and we were constantly on tours. When we were not performing, we were together looking at property or houses, going to Morrison's Cafeteria to eat every few days, going shopping, visiting Spring Hill (the farm), riding in the houseboat on the lake, working in our office or Billy Sherrill's offices at CBS, and the rest of the time we were writing songs. That's how we spent our days together. We had fun, but it all came to an end.

The demise of George and Tammy's marriage happened when things kept popping up between them, and George would start heavy drinking. Tammy was doing things to irritate him. Looking back, I believe Tammy had encouragement to rebuttal George. I believe it had its roots in a man, who was trying to manipulate Tammy into divorcing George, so he could have her for himself. He wanted Peanutt and me out of the way, so that he could get closer to Tammy.

I believe this man put his wife on the road with Tammy, and Tammy was naive to what was happening when she met and married Michael Tomlin after her divorce from George Jones. The wife that was touring with Tammy was the matron of honor at that wedding. Mysteriously, there was an end put to the Tammy and Michael Tomlin marriage. It only lasted a couple of months, and then who was left? She was the wife of the mystery man that was touring with Tammy.

Tammy suddenly became very sick while touring. She was making emergency trips from the shows where she was performing and flying back to Nashville to see her doctor. Tammy was leaving responsibilities with the wife to take care of the kids and handle everything until she could return from her doctor visits, and it didn't matter where she was located at the time. While Tammy was in Nashville to see the doctor, she was also seeing the husband of the woman that was out on the road with her and had been the matron of honor at her wedding to Mr. Tomlin.

The Country Music Awards were coming up. Tammy and her new love wanted to go to the Awards together, but they had a problem. The man was married, and his wife was a friend of Tammy's. So, what did they do? They announced to his wife that they were in love and were going to get married. The wife was devastated and hurt to the core because she truly idolized her husband. She felt betrayed by Tammy.

Tammy's friend and caretaker divorced her husband. With his wife out of the way, the master of the plan could now take a swing and hit his home run. He married Tammy Wynette and made her Mrs. George Richey. He got her, and he got control of her.

Like a hit man after his targets, Billy Sherrill was the next victim, and he was eliminated. During this melee, the ex-wife, who had been Tammy's caretaker, mysteriously died along with her pet dog, and "suicide" was the ruling of her untimely death. Little by little, Tammy Wynette was working for a new boss. Her new husband had everything under his control in her life. He was in total control of Tammy's productions, the publishing of her songs, her management, her caretaker, her medicine administrator, and he even became her banker and allowance giver. Tammy became his cash flow generator, but he was the owner and operator of Tammy

Wynette. Tammy was the one who lost the game, and then she simply died.

Tammy wasn't the only loser; her four daughters were next in line to take a beating. They were absolutely cheated out of everything rightfully theirs by their mother's death. No policies or papers of any kind could be found that gave them any rights to anything that belonged to Tammy Wynette. This was a disgrace and the worst case of greed that I have ever witnessed in my entire lifetime. Everything that Tammy had worked her butt off to generate her whole life went straight into the hands of her new husband.

A short while after Tammy's death, her ex-husband married a younger, healthier woman. This woman had also been Tammy's friend. Friend?? Friend in the same way that Mr. Master Planner George Ritchey had been George Jones' friend? The chips were on the table, the dice rolled, and we all lost.

Sometimes, I feel sorry for the children of the Jones/Wynette household. They were not unloved by their parents, but there was little time to spend with them growing up because of George and Tammy's busy schedule. The older three probably suffered more from lack of attention than Georgette did. Georgette was the baby, and she came along later in George and Tammy's life. Georgette was a rambunctious little girl once she started walking and wandering around the house.

I recall one incident in particular when George, Tammy, Peanutt, and I were sitting around the kitchen table on Tyne Boulevard playing a game of Aggravation. We had played several games before it dawned on Tammy that Georgette had not appeared in the kitchen for quite some time.

"Where's Georgette? I haven't seen her in a while," Tammy yelled.

She jumped up from the table and started looking for her. When Tammy found her daughter, she was hiding quiet as a mouse under a table in the living room.

"Georgette, what are you doing under there?" Tammy asked her.

Georgette didn't say a word. Tammy knew she had been up to something, so she started looking around to see what Georgette had been doing. Tammy noticed the cushions on the couch were not exactly in place. She started straightening up the cushions and turned one over to make it fit better. When she did, it had great big circles drawn on it with a black felt marker. Tammy turned over the rest of the cushions, and they were also marked up with the same circles. Tammy was furious. Georgette ruined a brand new very expensive living room suite that they purchased when they bought the Tyne Boulevard house.

Tammy began by telling Georgette to crawl out from under the table. Georgette just looked at Tammy and refused to move. Tammy called George into the living room and showed him the damage Georgette had done to the furniture.

"I'm going to bust her rear end!" Tammy yelled.

"No, you don't want to do that," George said. "Leave her alone. We can get another living room suite in here."

Tammy wasn't happy with George for not letting her spank Georgette, but she wouldn't go against him. She didn't spank her daughter Georgette, but she told her that if she ever did such a thing again, she would tear her butt up.

Tina felt a little left out at times. She was the baby of the family until Georgette came along. Tina loved Georgette, but Georgette made Tina feel secondary to her. When people came in, they oohed and ahhed over Georgette because she was the smallest and youngest child. Plus, she was a child bound to two stars. Tina found a way to rid her frustration. She'd do little things (sometimes big things) to get attention and upset Tammy. Even though it was in a mischievous way for a little kid, Tina got the job done,

Tammy had new drapes made for the house. She had just finished scolding Tina for something she did. Tammy then went about her business around the house. She assumed that Tina had been straightened out, and all was well. Tina wasn't of the same opinion, so she decided to retaliate. She got a pair of scissors and cut up the new drapes in the living room. Tammy discovered the ruined drapes, and she was beyond furious with her daughter. She knew Tina did the damage because Georgette was too small to handle the scissors, and Gwen and Jackie would not have done such a thing. Tammy called Tina out of her room and began to scold the fire out of her. George again stepped in and told Tammy not to berate her so harshly. Tammy threatened to beat the crap out of Tina, but George refused to let Tammy touch the child. He told Tammy to leave the child be.

Jackie was a cute little mama's girl. She was just old enough to adore her mother. She never raised a fuss about anything. She went along with whatever program Tammy had worked out. Jackie loved what time she got to spend with her mom. She was always very respectful of her mother's wishes, and Jackie was always smiling.

"Jackie's a very understanding girl; she's always easy to deal with," Tammy told me. "If I want something done, I can count on Jackie."

Tammy loved her girls, and I know that she would love to have had more time to spend with them, but her job was not like the lady's next door. Tammy's career demanded almost all of her time. Her schedule was deadly. She was out on the road for a month, home for a few days, had to squeeze in a recording session, carve out time for rehearsal with the band, take care of other business that had to be done, take time to listen to songwriters pitching new songs, and then do it all again the next month.

Gwen was a very pretty girl. She kept to herself because she was the oldest of the four and maybe she felt a responsibility to watch out for her siblings. She was very alert about what was taking place within the household. Gwen would stay clear of all the disagreements, she liked being in her room minding her own business, and at the same time, she kept a watchful eye as to who was doing what.

Tammy didn't spoil her girls, or at least not the way people normally define what a spoiled child is. Tammy made sure they had what they needed and made certain that someone was always there to take care of them while she was away from home. Tammy's mother was a real blessing to Tammy and the girls. Mildred was good to her grandchildren. She was stern and a bit old fashioned, but she made sure everyone stayed in line. She and her husband, Foy Lee, were very fine and sweet people. They were an asset to Tammy and George.

George loved those girls as well, and he looked out for them. George liked getting things for the girls that he knew they would like. He liked surprising his daughters with a special gift. Tammy was thoughtful in that way, too, but George always got a lot of good out of making someone happy with something the person didn't expect. That's a good quality in any man, but there aren't many that have that kind of spirit in them; especially, when it comes to stepchildren.

Peanutt, George Jones, Billy Sherrill, Sheila Richey (the wife and Tammy's caretaker), Tammy Wynette, Gwen Byrd, Jackie Byrd, Tina Byrd, Georgette Jones (George's adopted daughters), and I have been sorely wounded by Tammy's entire sordid extramarital affair. When this man faces Jesus Christ and tries to con his way into Glory-land, all hell will break loose outside the pearly gates.

George was the main victim of this conspiracy, and it's no wonder that he was so messed up during the last years of his marriage to Tammy. He tried every way imaginable to work things out with her, but nothing worked for him. George didn't suddenly get up one morning during the marriage and started drinking. He drank when she married him, and even though she didn't like it, she accepted it. Then all of a sudden, it was unforgivable. Why? She had a coach who encouraged her to take a hard stand with George. That coach knew exactly what would destroy George. George wanted to work things out with his wife, but the harder he tried, the more confused he became. George was knocked out of bounds and into pandemonium with no control over his life.

Cocaine became George's best friend, but he had no one

going to bat for him, and he caught all the turmoil of the ordeal. Someone calling himself a friend played up to his face while cutting his throat. If George Jones had not been a good man at heart, somebody could have been killed. George was in a state of mind that could have become violent for someone else, but his gentle, wholesome nature is what kept him from doing anything.

How do I, Charlene Montgomery, know all this? I was there when it happened, that's why. I saw the first sign of what was happening and coming at George and Tammy's house one night when we were all in their basement singing, playing the piano, writing song ideas down, and just clowning around. I saw something graphic, and I never said a word. I have never told anyone what I saw but believe me a light came on, and it wasn't long until their marriage was over. I don't blame George or Tammy. I blame the one who was behind the plan the entire time. George was in bad shape for long stretches. His mind was in hyper-overdrive, but he finally moved on and found happiness. Tammy remained trapped in a senseless warp of time and died a lonely and betrayed woman.

This is a song I wrote after Tammy died. I wrote it for George but never let him hear it.

She Lived With Him (But Died Loving Me)

We spent a few good years together
In perfect harmony
I thought that I belonged to her
and she was made for me
But someone else came along
played a sweeter melody
She lived with him
but died loving me

They spent the rest of her life together
for all the world to see
He thought their love was right on note
but I still held the key
They vowed til death do us part
that's how it turned out to be
She lived with him
but she died loving me

Our life together, it's not over
We share the same destiny
Someday we'll be together again
It will be for eternity
She's always been an angel
but her halo I failed to see
She lived with him
but she died loving me

She's now singing with the angels
in Heaven's jubilee
Soon I'll be joining her
she's waiting patiently
Once again we'll be together
the way it was meant to be
She lived with him
but died loving me

Tag: she lives with a man now, they both died loving me

Tammy and Al Gallico owned Altam Records. Since Peanutt wrote for Tammy's publishing company, she wanted him in Nashville so she, Peanutt, and George could write together. We spent a ton of time with them on the houseboat, in their home, and on their bus. We wrote songs constantly.

I only had one problem about moving to Nashville. I had a daughter who was in grade school in Florence. I had someone, who babysat with her while we went to and from Nashville but in Nashville, I didn't have anyone to help me with her. When I told Tammy my problem, she said it was no big deal. She said that True could stay with her girls at her house, and either her mom or the housekeeper would take care of her.

"True will love my girls, and they will love having her here," she said. "We'll enroll her in Franklin Road Academy where my girls go to school, and that will be no problem at all for anybody."

So that's what we did. Tammy's girls were very good to True; especially, Tina who was about the same age.

Tammy's housekeeper was a very sweet black lady. I'll never forget her calling one day and asking to speak to Peanutt.

"Mr. Peanutt, Tammy is mad at Mr. George, and she left. Now he's come home and he's plumb drunk. You come and get him out of here, Sir, I have these here children, and I can't handle no drunk man."

We knew she meant business, so we took off to Tyne Boulevard. When we got to the door, she met us.

"Mr. Peanutt," she said in a frantic voice, "Get that man out of here right now. He's so drunk, he don't know where he is."

Peanutt told Miss Doris to calm down. Peanutt grabbed George, we took him with us, and we kept him until he sobered up.

Peanutt and I had more time to spend with True than Tammy did with her girls. When we got home and off the road, we didn't have as much business to take care of as Tammy and George did. We would always take True home with us at night when we left Tammy and George's house, and then take her to school in the morning. Whoever picked up Tammy's kids also picked up True from school if we were with George and Tammy on the road.

This was the way life had to be if you were in the music business. You had to have a system, and you had to make it work. The demand on the life of the artist is great. You either go along with the program or you lose out. Maybe the children didn't quite understand the whole thing in their younger years, but as they grew older and had children of their own (including True), they seemed to have a better outlook on their childhood.

Yes, it robbed them of time they desperately needed and wanted with their parents, but at the same time, it also provided them with beautiful homes, playgrounds, and luxuries they would not have otherwise had. It's an honor to have famous parents.

CHAPTER TWELVE

Billy Sherrill -
Founder of Tammy Wynette

There were two major assets Tammy Wynette had that made her a big star. She possessed an unusually beautiful voice, and she had one of the greatest producers in the music business in Billy Sherrill. There are thousands of singers in the world that have good voices, but they never had the producer. Tammy did. Only an idiot would say that Billy Sherrill was anything less than a genius. Why? Billy possessed the wisdom and knowledge to prove himself to the world by his abilities rather than his words.

It has been said over and over that Billy was shy, quiet, reserved, had few friends, and did not socialize with his artists. Billy was all business. He was a lot of fun to be around, but he was cautious about how he conducted himself, and it was obvious that he was not trying to impress anyone.

Peanutt told me stories about Billy before I was ever introduced to him, so I had already formed my opinions of him. I liked him and was anxious to meet him. Peanutt and Billy were in a band called, "The Fairlanes" when they were teenagers. Peanutt told funny stories about Billy. He told me that at one point in Billy's life, he was not too fond of dogs; especially, those that chased after cars. Sometimes Billy would open the car door and knock the dog out of the way. Peanutt said that Billy would not always participate in some of the things he and the rest of the band would do, and that made me think that Billy was probably smarter than the rest of the bunch.

Peanutt was friends with Tom Stafford, who was also a songwriter and owned a publishing company and a small recording studio, which was located on Tennessee Street in Florence. It was situated in the upstairs of The City Drug Store, which was operated by Tom's parents. Billy, Peanutt, Rick Hall, Donnie Fritts, and a gang of other musicians and songwriters hung out at Tom's place. They all liked Tom Stafford.

Tom was another person who was different. He was the kind of person who was easy to get along with but was very strange. For example, Tom asked Peanutt and me to spend the day with him, so we did. The very next day, Tom called and asked us to come back over to his house. By the time we got there, he would not even answer his door for us. About two hours later, Tom called back and wanted us to come back over to his place. Tom was a very private person, but he loved having the association with all the music people.

When I finally got to meet Billy Sherrill, I was surprised. I had told several people in Nashville that the one person I wanted to meet was Billy. I was told that he was extremely arrogant. I met Billy after Peanutt started writing for Tammy's publishing company, Altam that she and Al Gallico owned. We were in Billy's office quite often pitching songs to Billy, George, and Tammy. Then on many occasions we were in the studio at Columbia when they would be recording. Billy was always there since he was the producer. I was a little bit nervous around Billy at first because of all the warnings I had been given about him, but I found Billy very nice, and he never made me feel uncomfortable. I went with Peanutt to his office and to the sessions and Billy never seemed conceited or arrogant to me.

I'll never forget one day when we were in the studio doing a session with Tammy and George. Billy came over to the little sitting area at Columbia and asked me for a dime. There was a coke machine that required a dime for a cup of coke. What made me feel good was the fact that he wasn't too proud to ask me for the money. I felt like he was comfortable around me. Another time, he asked me for a cigarette. Once he scolded me because right in the middle of a recording, I flipped a Zippo cigarette lighter open, and the sound picked up on the tape. He simply asked that we keep the noise down while he was recording. He didn't know who did it, but it was I. To me, that was not being arrogant, Billy was doing what he had to do, and it was my fault because I should have known better.

"Why do women like Charlie Rich over Waylon Jennings?" Billy asked me one day. "It looks to me like women would like Waylon better."

"Women like Charlie because of his hair," I explained, "and they don't like Waylon because of his hair. Waylon's hair looks like he just came out from under a greasy vehicle."

Billy died laughing. I meant that Waylon looked more like an auto mechanic than a recording artist. Charlie was suave. Once, Billy asked me if I had ever tasted a drink called, "Sambuca." I told him no because I didn't drink. He insisted on taking Peanutt and me out to eat one time after one of Tammy's recording sessions. He wanted me to try this drink, Sambuca. We went inside with Billy, and he ordered the drink for me. One of the drink's features was coffee beans in the bottom of the glass. I loved the taste of it. I am not a drinker, but I told Billy that if I were, the Sambuca would be my favorite drink.

Billy was not conceited or arrogant. He was reserved, and I'd say choosy of his associations and to me, that makes him a wise person. Billy most likely got his reputation because he didn't yoke himself up with every Tom, Dick, and Harry he came in contact with. Billy was a serious businessman. He knew the do's and don'ts of the business world as well as music. He didn't have to act goofy to get attention. He didn't need attention and frankly didn't want attention. Billy was serious about his artists. He spent time knowing who his artists were, and what they were about. He studied their characteristics, so he would better know how to deal with each of them. He was concerned about their careers, and he only wanted the best for them.

Billy once told me that it would hurt him to lose his artists; and especially, Tammy Wynette. Tanya Tucker had just left him, and he said that really did hurt him. He couldn't stand the thoughts of losing George or Tammy, but he did.

Tammy would have stayed with Billy forever had it not been for her new husband, George Richey. George Richey was also a producer, songwriter, piano player, and publisher. Tammy had become his wife. He felt he should be able to control who her producer would be because she was his wife. Tammy left Billy Sherill and George Richey began producing Tammy. It was disastrous for Tammy's career. There were no records of Tammy anywhere. You could go to Walmart, music stores, truck stops, and anywhere they sold records, but Tammy Wynette records were nowhere to be found. I couldn't believe that an artist as hot as Tammy didn't have any records on the market to be purchased. I think leaving Billy was the biggest mistake she ever made in her life, and I think Tammy knew it.

Tammy and Billy Sherrill. She told me many times that she'd never leave him. She always spoke so highly of him and praised him for what he had done for her. I felt that there was a bond between Tammy and Billy, and that all the King's horses and all the King's men could never tear them apart. Evidently, there was a stronger force behind her than what I had anticipated. That same force tore down every aspect of her stunning career and went on to literally destroy her life. Billy knew what was going to happen even before it happened. When George Jones and Tammy split, it ruined everything. There was a family-type atmosphere around Billy's office when Billy, Tammy, George, Narrow Wilson, Carmel Taylor, George Richey, Sheila Richey, Peanutt, and me would get together. We'd all gather in Billy's office and pitch our songs. It was a pleasant and happy time for everyone.

After the trouble with George and Tammy, it was all messed up. There were those who sided with Tammy, and those who sided with George. It was hard to be mutual friends with all involved. You either had to be on George's side or Tammy's. If you were on Tammy's side, you could have nothing to do with those who associated with George. There was a great separation created among the whole family of associates, and it hurt everyone involved, and eventually hurt Billy as well.

Tammy told me that she would see to it that an Earl (Peanutt) Montgomery song would never get cut by Billy Sherrill or anybody else where she had influence. She was mad at Peanutt for taking up with George after they split up. Tammy failed to realize that Peanutt had known both Billy and George before she ever came on the scene. Peanutt didn't care if he got a song cut or not; he was not turning his back on George regardless of the consequences. Peanutt loved Tammy and always praised her for her talent as well as her tolerance of George. Peanutt has said many times that Tammy was the most graceful lady he had ever known. Tammy didn't try to sell her body with sexy movements; she didn't have to. Tammy Wynette sold her talent. She had what people wanted because it came from her heart. How can anybody knock what she did? She was total success!

Tammy was also a very good person. She was from the country, and her country roots showed up from time to time. She also had a classiness about her that would make some people think she'd only been raised on the streets of New York City. George Jones was the same way. He was also from the country but was very classy in his own way. He chose to be down to earth and different than most country music stars. George only wanted to be himself. Tammy sometimes liked the feeling of knowing she was a star. Other times, she couldn't believe who she actually was.

Billy Sherrill never seemed any different every time I met him. He was always neatly dressed, clean-shaven, and looked the role of a true professional. I appreciated what I saw in Billy. Some of the people in the music business literally made me sick. They couldn't get anything done without the help of alcohol, pills, and sleeping around. I noticed that after a session, Billy was finished working with music for the day. He didn't go hanging out at the bars with the artists and songwriters. He'd have other plans. I've never seen him out of line in any kind of way in all the years I was around him. He was really respectful to the people he associated with. He might acknowledge that he knew a person was there, and he might not. He was capable of walking right by you and never saying hello. That was Billy's disposition. Those who didn't know him might take that as an insult, or that he was conceited or strange. I took it as a man who was there on business, and his job was all he had on his mind. He didn't have time for the nonsense. Billy had no apologies to make. He was definitely smart and had been extremely successful. It all paid off for him whatever flavor someone wants to call him.

Billy Sherill is one of my favorite people in the music business. I like his disposition, I like his way of doing business, and I like the very things that people told me I wouldn't like about him. He was always interesting. He had very few words to say, but when he did speak, it had real meaning. He could sometimes be what you call, "cocky," but that all came with his clever mind. One never knew exactly what Billy was thinking but if he heard something he liked, he'd jump on it with all focus. He didn't hesitate to make a move on an idea that struck him just right. He knew what he liked and he'd go after it. Billy knew when something was right on the money. That's what made him the producer, musician, and songwriter he was. If I was a recording artist wanting to make it in the music business, I'd feel cheated if I couldn't have Billy Sherrill as my producer. If I was looking for a song, I'd want a song written by Billy Sherrill, and I'd want a Billy Sherrill contract behind me. Billy Sherrill spells success. He was the best.

....

CHAPTER THIRTEEN

Short Stories That Will Live Long

It was a cold December day, and Christmas was just around the corner. Peanutt and I were at George and Tammy's house on Tyne Boulevard. We were in a discussion about the economy. Gas prices had just increased to seventy-cents a gallon from twenty-five cents a gallon at some stations. It was quite an increase from where the price of gas had been. George told Tammy that it looked like they would need to get a small car that would be easy on gas and proceeded to remind her that every vehicle they owned was a gas-guzzler. After discussing this for a while, Tammy had agreed that it wouldn't be a bad idea. George made the remark that if gas went any higher, the dealerships would raise the prices on small cars because there would be a great demand for them. It all made good sense to us.

We decided to play a game of Aggravation. The four of us were sitting around the glass-top table in the eating area of the kitchen. George didn't seem as interested in the game as he usually was.

"What's on your mind, George?" Tammy asked him.

"Aww," he said, "I was just thinking about nothing in particular."

Tammy put on a pot of ham and dumplings. When we finished the game, George pushed himself from the table.

"Peanutt, come with me, I want you to ride to town with me."

I didn't really want them to go off together, but I thought since Tammy was cooking I couldn't leave her. Tammy and I stayed home, and George and Peanutt went to town. While they were gone, George told Peanutt that he wanted to find Tammy a Vega station wagon. That's what he wanted to get his wife for Christmas. Peanutt assured George he'd find her one. George said that once he found it, he would buy it and wanted Peanutt to keep it until Christmas morning and then bring it to their house.

When Peanutt and George returned home, we had dinner ready for them. We all sat down at the table to eat. George kept looking at me and smiling. Peanutt was acting a little anxious. They both appeared to have been up to something.

"Peanutt," I said, "Where did you and George go?"

"I knew that was coming," George quipped.

"We just went looking around." Peanutt commented.

"Peanutt, go ahead and give it to her, there ain't no need in waiting till Christmas," George told him.

"Oh my goodness," I thought, *"there's no telling what they have done."*

Peanutt reached into his coat pocket and pulled out a small bag. He slowly opened the bag and handed me a ring box. I opened it right there at the table with George, Tammy, and Peanutt watching me. I thought I'd faint. It was a gorgeous three-carat diamond ring. It was the most beautiful ring I had ever laid my eyes on. I could not believe that Peanutt would buy such an expensive ring for me.

"Peanutt, this had to cost a lot of money," I said.

"Yes, it did. I was going to get a smaller one, but George wanted me to get this one for you. It was the one he picked out."

I turned to George. "Thank you too, George, I absolutely love it. There's not a ring in the world that I would like better." I was shocked. I loved that ring.

After we left, Peanutt told me what George had planned to get Tammy for Christmas.

"I've got to get on the phone and locate her a Vega station wagon," Peanutt said.

He found one in Athens, Alabama. We drove over to look at it. It was a light tan color. We called George and told him about it, and he told us to tell the dealership to consider it sold. They held the car for George. Peanutt and I took the money to the dealership, bought the car, and kept it until Christmas morning. We fastened huge yellow ribbons to the car and tied some of the ribbon into a bow to make a present. We pulled it in the driveway early Christmas morning before they got up. When Tammy saw the car, she didn't know exactly what to say.

When Tammy saw the car in her driveway she commented, "Well, that one will be easy on gas, and it will be great to take the kids back and forth to school and to run around town in."

She was totally surprised with her gift.

George could be a schemer when he wanted to be. He could pull off just about anything he wanted anytime he wanted. He would find a way to get the job done. I liked the look on his face when he did something for somebody, and he surprised the person with it. His expression showed that he always enjoyed doing things for others, and he liked to watch the other person's reaction.

When they lived at the Landing in Hendersonville, Tennessee, Tammy and I had gone shopping for the afternoon. When we started home, Tammy started trembling.

"Just look at me, I'm shaking!" she exclaimed.

"What's wrong Tammy?" I asked her.

"George has been up to something, I just know he has. I feel it in my bones," She explained.

"What are you saying?" I questioned.

"When I get like this, I'm usually right, and I know he's been up to something."

We had driven George's car to town. When we pulled into their driveway, there was an unfamiliar car parked there. Tammy's El Dorado was nowhere to be seen.

"My car's not here; I wonder whose car that is?" she said while looking and peering around the premises.

We grabbed our bags, exited the car, and went in the house. George was sitting on the couch and grinning from ear to ear.

"Well, how do you like your new car? I traded your El Dorado in on that one," George enthusiastically asked.

We went outside to inspect this new ride George bought. It was a Lincoln. At that time, it was popular for people in the music business to trade in their Cadillac's and buy Lincoln's.

"Oh, I really like it, it's really nice," Tammy replied.

She thanked George for getting her the new car, and I could tell her excitement was anything but genuine.

After we went inside the house, George and Peanutt went down to the deck to hang out.

"Crap!" Tammy yelled. "I loved my Eldorado. I haven't had it very long, and I loved my car. Now it's gone, and I'm stuck with this one. That burns me up, but I can't let George know because it would hurt his feelings, and he'd probably pull a drunk if he thought I didn't like it."

"Tammy, it's a beautiful car," I told her.

"Yeah it is, but I've always liked Cadillacs and especially Eldorados. Well, I might as well drive it and accept it now." She reasoned. George never knew how Tammy really felt about his surprise.

A story I love to tell is what happened on one of our trips to the Bahamas. We were staying with George and Tammy at their beautiful summerhouse in Lakeland, Florida, and it happened to be Peanutt's birthday, February 6th.

"I've got an idea," George said. "It's Peanutt's birthday, so let's take a trip to the Bahamas!"

We were all in agreement with that suggestion. Bill and Patsy Sledge were also in Florida so George invited them to go with us. George and Tammy had been doing some TV commercials for Babcock Furniture. George called their good friends, Cliff and Maxine, who lived in Lakeland, Florida and asked them to go. The entourage suddenly swelled to four couples making the trip, and in a few days we headed to Miami to board the Flavia Cruise Liner.

It turned out that we were in the Bahamas on Valentine's Day. Trying to figure out how to occupy our time, the men decided they would leave the women and go do their own thing. That left the four women to decide what they would do for the day.

We decided to sun bathe, so we changed to our bikinis. We went up to the captain's deck because it was more private. Nobody was supposed to be on that deck except the Captain and crew, but we didn't mind breaking the rules. We stretched out on our lounge chairs, and I had unfastened my bra strap while lying on my stomach. I fell asleep and while sleeping, I turned over on my back.

I was sleeping really soundly when somebody yelling at me suddenly awakened me.

"Charlene, wake up, your top is gone!" Tammy yelled. She happened to look over at me, and I was totally exposed without a stitch covering me.

It scared me to death. She happened to look over at me, and I was completely topless. I was beyond embarrassed. I covered my breasts with my hands while we looked for the top that wasn't anywhere near me. We found it wrapped around a pole and almost ready to blow into the ocean.

"Tammy, I'm proud we are on the captain's deck cause nobody saw me but you girls!" I exclaimed.

"Oh, yes they have, look over yonder at that other ship." Maxine pointed out.

There were at least a half-dozen men dressed in red coats, white shirts, and black bow ties. They were standing in the windows with binoculars looking straight at us, and what a view they had! I grabbed my towel and beach bag and ran off the deck as fast as I could while the girls were almost doubled over laughing.

I told the girls I'd hate them forever if they told Peanutt and George what had happened, and they agreed to keep the incident a secret.

"I wonder what the men have been up to," Tammy said while we were walking to our rooms.

"It's Valentine's Day," I replied.

"Oh, yeah, that's right," Tammy said. "George better not forget."

"Peanutt and I don't celebrate Valentine's Day anymore," I told them.

"I know Bill won't get me anything." Patsy exclaimed.

"There's no danger that Cliff won't remember, either," Maxine said.

"Let's all go to the staff in the restaurant and talk them into baking us a heart-shaped cake and have them deliver it to our table tonight at dinner," I told them.

Everybody liked my idea, so we headed to the kitchen. We told the chef to be sure to write, *To the ladies* on top of the cake. The chef was happy to oblige and assured us he would make sure our plan would be carried out.

True to what we ladies knew for sure would happen, every one of the men had forgotten it was Valentine's Day, and of course we mentioned nothing about it to them. That night at dinner, the waiter came to the table with our cake. The white cake with red letters that said, *To the ladies* was highlighted with burning candles that made it a stunningly beautiful cake.

We acted completely and pleasantly surprised.

"Which of you boys did this for us?" I asked.

Peanutt didn't say anything because he would never have thought of the idea in the first place. Bill said it wasn't him, and Cliff also said he didn't do it. George took a long breath, straightened up in his chair and had a proud look on his face.

"Well, y'all thought we had forgotten about Valentine's Day, didn't you?" George exclaimed dripping with syrup.

George figured one of the other men had done it and didn't want us to know who, so he went along with the program and claimed the credit.

"What do you think about us now? We're not so bad after all are we?" George asked.

Tammy was real antsy and started squirming in her seat. She pounded the table with her fist.

"George Jones," she yelled while beating the table. "Don't you dare take the credit for that cake; you didn't have it made, and you know it. I know who did, and it was none of you. Y'all forgot about us, and we knew you would, so we went to the kitchen and had a cake baked for ourselves!"

George looked like a plucked chicken. I felt a little sorry for him because I knew he was trying to make us all feel good. We all laughed about it later because we were just having fun at the expense of our husbands. What Tammy would never let me live down was losing my top and becoming a peep show for several google-eyed men.

One evening, we were all in a motel room in Nashville. We had been up late every night getting prepared for George's recording session the next day. George, Peanutt, and several other people were lounging in the room. They were making plans for the night.

"I'm going to bed, good night," I said.

George yelled out, "Alright!"

"If you all want me to go to bed that badly," I said, "I'll just stay right here and see what's going on?"

Everybody in the room started laughing. I didn't catch on, so I thought about what I said.

"No, I didn't mean it that way," I explained.

George was laughing so hard. He loved to get the best of me whenever he could find the opportunity.

Tammy called Peanutt and me one time when we were living in Florence and asked us to come up to Nashville and get George. She said George was drunk, and she wanted us to come and get him. Peanutt told Tammy we would be there. She said he was at home and couldn't leave because she had hidden all the keys. She knew George wouldn't go off without a car.

When we arrived at the Tyne Boulevard house, George was there. He wasn't drunk but very close. Peanutt had asked Bob

Tidwell, a friend of ours, to ride along with us. After we were there for a little while, George decided to go home with us, but he wanted me to fix his hair first.

I was combing George's hair, Peanutt had gone to the bathroom, and Bob was sitting at the table with George and me. The comb slipped out of my hand and fell to the floor. When I bent over to pick up the comb, George pinched me on the rear. I didn't think anything about it because George was just being ornery.

When we were ready to leave for Florence, Peanutt said to me: "Charlene, you let George ride with you, and Bob and I will ride together."

After we arrived at our house in Florence, Peanutt was laughing and telling George and me about what Bob had said to him on the way home.

"Peanutt," Bob said. "I don't know how to say this to you, but you had better watch your back with that George. While you were in the bathroom, George pinched Charlene on her butt."

Peanutt said that Bob was dead serious. Peanutt told him that it was just George cutting up, and that he didn't mean a thing by it. Bob said that he wouldn't want another man to pinch his wife on the butt. Peanutt assured Bob that he'd just have to know George to understand him, and that George would have done the same thing if it had been his sister combing his hair.

George loved to clown around. I was at the Brooks Acres house one day. We were all down on the deck fishing. Just as I pulled back my rod to cast, George caught my reel, grabbed the fishing line, and put the hook in the bottom of my swimsuit. I couldn't get it loose, and he was laughing so hard tears were rolling down his cheeks. He loved to pull mischievous pranks.

Another time, we were visiting George and Tammy when they lived in Hendersonville. Tammy saw a mouse run across the floor, and she was so frightened. She went on and on about how badly it scared her. About four days later, I decided to pull a prank on her. I went to the novelty store and bought a toy rat. It was a wind up model and had real gray fur that made it look real. I found the opportunity to sneak into her bedroom. I placed the mouse about half way down in the bed on the side where Tammy slept. I positioned it, so it wouldn't unwind until she lifted the cover off of the rat's winding stem.

Tammy went to bed. She straightened out her legs and released the blankets that were holding the rat and keeping it from activating. Suddenly, the little rat started running all over her bed. She kicked off the covers, jumped out of the bed, got up in a chair, screamed at the top of her lungs, and then started throwing her wigs at the mouse. She was yelling at George to kill it.

George knew about it, and he played along. When the rat finally wound down, it laid there like it was dead. Tammy thought George had killed it. When she finally discovered it was a prank, Tammy got madder than the devil at me. She phoned me after she calmed down a little and told me she was going to get even. George told me how hard it was for him not to laugh at her, but he knew he couldn't. It would have made her furious if she knew that George was in on the prank because it scared her so badly. We all laughed about it later, and I couldn't help but chuckle when I thought about her warning me that she'd catch up to me.

Tammy was not innocent when it came to pulling her own pranks on people. She loved to get a laugh at somebody else's expense. She was a lot of fun when everything was going smoothly in her life. I wouldn't take anything for the good times we had with her. I loved to hear her laugh and tell funny stories about different entertainers. She'd tell funny stories about Jan Howard, Loretta Lynn, Dottie West, and Tanya Tucker. She loved those ladies and talked about them all the time as her favorite female artists. Tammy's favorite male artists were Don Gibson and Charlie McCoy. She absolutely loved Charlie. She was loyal to the people she liked but if she didn't care for you, you better keep your distance.

I'll never forget the day we went shopping at Kmart to buy George a pair of jeans. Tammy found a pair she really liked. The jeans featured one purple and one orange back pockets. I thought to myself, *"Surely you're not going to buy those for George."* I knew George would not wear those pants, but I didn't make a comment because she thought they were really cool.

"What the hell is this?" George said when she handed him the jeans. "Do you really think I'm going to wear those things?"

"You go buy your own jeans from now on because I can't ever please you," Tammy said with an aggravation in her tone.

"Believe me, I will," George replied.

It was little things like this that irritated George and Tammy and turned into bigger matters that kept them from getting along.

I always knew when George was deep in thought about something he was wanting to do, thinking about something he didn't like, or how to do something that was on his mind he didn't want to talk about. He had a quirky habit that always tipped me off when he had something up his sleeve. He'd suck air through the sides of his teeth. He never knew I had him figured out.

"George is up to something," I'd tell Peanutt and then told him how I knew it. Peanutt started paying attention to George's habit and just like clockwork, every time we'd hear George swish air through the sides of his mouth, he'd wind up pulling something off before the day was through. He would do it a lot of times when we were out riding around or doing something just to be passing time. George was pretty easy to figure out if you knew him well.

Tammy could read him like a book. She'd sometimes say to me, "I want you and Peanutt to spend the night; I think George is restless."

Peanutt and I would spend the night and play cards or Aggravation in order to keep his mind off whatever he was thinking. Peanutt would sometimes come up with a song idea and we'd get to work on that. Peanutt was good with George. He never wanted George and Tammy upset at each other. He really liked Tammy and highly respected her. He thought they were perfect for each other. They really were but didn't realize it.

Sue Richards was my best friend, and we spent a lot of time together. One night she called me,

"Charlene, I'm coming to get you. George and Jimmy are off together, and I found out that they're at the Tourway Inn."

"Okay, come on and pick me up, and I'll go with you," I answered.

A few minutes later, Sue pulled in my driveway, and we went to the Tourway Inn. We found that they had indeed checked in. Sue went to the room, and there were some women inside. Sue was furious with Jimmy. George and Jimmy were drinking. Jimmy tried to reason with Sue, but she was too angry to hear anything he had to say.

"Sue, George is the one with the women; I just brought him out here. I didn't know anything about any women being here." Jimmy cried.

Sue pulled off her shoe and started slapping the fire out of Jimmy with it. She threatened a couple of the women as well. All the while, Jimmy was trying to explain that he only took George where he wanted to go, and this is what happened.

Jimmy dumped George at the Tourway Inn and went home. I had never seen Sue that upset. George was probably pulling one of his pranks on Jimmy to get him in hot water. I told Sue that George would do things like that just to make Jimmy squirm. I helped to get her cooled down and off Jimmy's back. There was always something George was pulling on one of us.

Peanutt was not a person who pulled pranks very often. He was always afraid he'd make somebody really mad at him, so for the most part he stayed away from that kind of trouble.

Linda, my sister, who George later married, would mispronounce words that would make George correct her. She'd say things like "reality company" instead of realtors. She'd say, "George, do you need an alka-sucker?" George really got a kick out of it. He actually thought she didn't know any better.

One time, George bought a Nudie suit. He dressed up wearing it and his new Nudie boots. He walked out of the bedroom and asked Linda how he looked?

"Oh, George, you look sharper than a tick," she replied.

"Sharper than a what?" he asked.

"Sharper than a tick." she said again.

I think that one actually upset George. Linda knew that the word was "tack," but she wanted to see George get flustered with her. It was these little things that made friendship with George a lot of fun. Some folks thought we were all as wild as a herd of buffalos, but we did it all in fun. It made memories that will never be forgotten. That was the good part of it all.

One of Peanutt's favorite stories is about a fishing trip we took with George and Linda.

One day, George decided we would all go fishing. We grabbed rods, reels, and tackle, and took off down to McFarland Park on the Tennessee River. The fish were not biting too well that day, but George caught a small bass. He got excited and told Peanutt that if we wanted to catch fish, we needed to get into the middle of the river. George had a brainstorm.

"Peanutt, let's go to Russell Sporting Goods and buy us a boat, so we can get out there where the fish are."

George wasted no time. We all four piled in the car and went looking for a boat. Before the day was gone, George had a boat and then realized he had no way to pull it. We drove to Bobby Mitchell Chevrolet on Florence Blvd. and bought a new truck. We pulled the boat back to the river but by the time we made it there, it was nearly dark. We had no place to stay the night, so George decided what he needed was a camper.

"I tell you what, Peanutt, let's just go home tonight, and tomorrow we'll go get us a camper."

We went home. The next day Peanutt and George went shopping for a camper and ended up with a super nice motor home.

"Peanutt and I are on the way down to the river with the

motor home." George said when he called Linda and me. "Go tell Wild Bill to come get the boat and trailer and pull it down to McFarland Park. I want you and Charlene to run to town and get exactly what I tell you on this list."

He gave us a list a mile long. It consisted of a grill, charcoal, food, etc. When we had finished shopping, we tallied up over three hundred dollars for supplies. We were all set up to camp and very well prepared for a fishing spree, a cook out, and a good time. George was right. The fish were further out in the river. We caught a stringer full of fish, had a good meal, and played cards that night inside George's new motor home.

"Go down there and tie the boat up to a tree," George told Peanutt when we were done fishing for the day.

Peanutt secured the boat just as he was commanded, and we went to bed after playing cards. During the night, it began to rain heavily. The sudden downpour caused the river to rise very rapidly. Because the boat had been tied to a tree, it couldn't rise with the water.

The next morning, George, Peanutt, and Wild Bill found the boat completely under water but still tied to the tree. After the men got the water out of the boat and cleaned it up, George was done with it all and announced he was going home.

As soon as we got in the house, George called a friend, Ralph May, and offered to sell him the boat, trailer, and the truck for about two-thirds of what he had paid for it. Ralph bought it.

That's the way George was. He was impulsive and would settle for nothing less than what he wanted at the moment. By the next day, he wouldn't want it at all. Peanutt reminded George that the fishing trip was awful, expensive, and ended in disaster.

George replied, "It's just money, Peanutt. We had a good time, and it was worth it to me." It never bothered George if he spent money and made deals other people thought were wasteful and stupid.

....

CHAPTER FOURTEEN

Linda (Welborn) (Jones) Dodson
Wife Number Four
(Written by Linda Jones)

"I personally want to tell you about myself, Linda Carolyn (Green) (Welborn) (Jones) Dodson. Some of the books that have been written about George Jones and Tammy Wynette have all but chewed me up and spit me out. Even though I will have to pay thanks to George, he never put me down in any of the books. Of course, George knew me, and he knew that a lot of what has been said is not the truth. I realize that some people will do or say anything to gain a few brownie points with someone they're trying to get close to or impress.

I will tell the truth in this chapter, and I hope I don't hurt anybody. I'm not writing this portion of the book to get back at anybody. I don't have anything to gain or anything to lose, and I'm not being paid any money. I simply want the truth to be known. I was born in Marion County, Alabama on August 8, 1948. My parents are James Alvin and Irene Green. I was the fifth child of their nine children. There were four before me and four after me. I guess I have always been stuck in the middle. My dad went to work at Reynolds Metal Company in 1947. When I was six years old, we moved to Muscle Shoals, Alabama and that's where I spent my younger years.

I started school at Howell Graves School in Muscle Shoals. I wasn't what you'd call a real country girl. I have always lived in the city limits. I have never lived on a farm, but we did have animals to take care of. I had chores just like people that did live in the country. My mother never had a job outside of the home. She was too busy sewing, cooking, and cleaning. My dad believed in working hard and each child was expected to do chores around the home.

Every cotton crop owner in the county would come to our house and ask daddy to let us children pick or chop cotton for them. They knew how hard daddy worked and made us work. They knew we were healthy kids and were able to do a good job for them. We were not too happy that they thought that much of us, but daddy took it as a real compliment. He was big on wanting his children to always be ready and willing to help anybody out that needed help.

Our family was not what you would consider poor people. We just lived like we were poor kids. Daddy saved half of his weekly paychecks and put it in savings. We lived off of the other half, and the extra money he'd pick up from odd jobs. My mother was a Christian lady. We went to church every time the doors were open. She would not let us miss a service, come rain, hail, sleet, or snow, we went to church.

I enrolled in high school at Colbert County High School in Leighton, Alabama. It was there that I met Douglas Howard Welborn. Doug and I dated while we were in school together, and then married when I was seventeen years old. Doug was only eighteen. We got married on November 25, 1965. Soon after Doug and I married, we moved to Chicago, Illinois. It was kind of hard on me for I had never been away from home. My dad was really strict on us kids and would hardly let us spend the night away from home even with relatives.

Doug and I both got good jobs in Chicago. We were both making good money and were doing just fine. I worked for Motorola, and Doug worked for Bradfoot Gear. After almost five years had passed, I finally got pregnant with my first child. Howard Dale Welborn was born on October 15, 1970. I quit my job with Motorola to take care of Dale. I waited until Dale was old enough to be put in daycare before I went back to work. Then I went to work

for Western Electric as a punch press operator. Doug and I started
going to church. We became very involved in church work; we had
both become Christians. We decided we wanted to attend a Semi-
nary to learn more about the Bible and the ministry. We enrolled
in the Moody Bible College and were as happy as any two people
could be.

Later on Doug got involved with a group of young believers.
They didn't go to our church, but they held their meetings in their
homes. They were a nondenominational group. They called any
place they decided to meet their church. Sometimes their meetings
would last until two or three o'clock in the morning. I had never
heard of such a group before. I had always been a Baptist and had
always attended church in a church house. Doug totally believed in
the young believers, but I refused to get involved with them. I never
felt that they were religious at all, in fact, I felt like their group was
a cult. I tried desperately to convince Doug to get away from them
and start back to our church, but he flat refused. I had gone as far as
I could go with the situation.

I could no longer deal with Doug and the group of people
he was involved with. I realized I had to do something about it. The
more I complained to Doug, the more he resented me. We started
having serious problems over the situation. It had gotten to where
we hardly even spoke to each other. I finally decided I couldn't
live with it any longer. Doug went to work one morning, and I
packed some clothes for Dale and me and took a few toys for Dale,
a blanket and a pillow, and left the rest of our possessions behind.
I left Doug a note and told him that I hated that our marriage had
come to this point, but I was leaving him. I had worked just as hard
as Doug, made just as much money as Doug, paid as much for our
possessions, but I left it all behind.

I went to Liberty, South Carolina, a little town west of
Greenville to live with my sister Paulene Thomas and her husband
Jamie. A little while after I got there, I got a job at Libco Mills, a
carpet plant, where Paulene and Jamie worked. I was doing just fine

and getting ready to get my own place. Then one day the doorbell rang. It was Doug.

"I've come to get Dale," he said.

I told him no way I was going to let Dale go back to Chicago.

"Well, I'll just wait until you go back to work, and I'll get him while you're gone to work," he commented.

"No you won't because I'll not go back to work." I replied.

I stayed at home until I knew Doug had left town. When I did go back to my job, I didn't have a job. After I realized I was without a job, I decided to move back home to Muscle Shoals, Alabama. My dad had just passed away at fifty-four years old with a massive heart attack, and my mother was forty-nine years old, and she needed me with her. Dale and I moved in with mother. I filed for a divorce from Doug as soon as I got to Muscle Shoals. I didn't ask for anything, no alimony, no child support, and not any of the possessions we had accumulated during our marriage. All I wanted was the divorce papers signed.

Doug had asked me to come back to him, and I asked him in return if he would get away from that bunch of so-called Christians and he said, "I can't promise you that."

"Okay, then it's forever over for me and you," I told him.

That's when I made up my mind that I wanted the divorce. Our divorce became final in 1974. All I got was custody of Dale, and that's all I wanted. Doug had visiting rights. I had only been at my mother's for a couple of weeks when one day the phone rang. It was my sister Charlene Montgomery calling me.

"Hey Linda," she said. "I want you to come over to my house. Peanutt's brother Aaron is here from Peoria, Illinois, and he has just gotten a divorce and is having a hard time with it, and I'd like to introduce you to him. He's real nice, and I think he'd feel better if he just had someone to talk to."

"Well, I'll come by in a little while," I replied.

I think Charlene was also thinking that I needed to get out of the house as well. I had not done anything since I'd been at mother's house. I went to Charlene's, and she introduced me to Aaron Montgomery. He was a nice looking man, very neat and well dressed. Aaron was very polite and well mannered, and I really liked him. Peanutt and some other guy were sitting in the den playing the guitar and singing. They didn't seem to be interested in anything except what they were doing.

Charlene finally asked me to come to the den and wanted to introduce me to the other man. Peanutt looked up at me and said,

"Linda, this is my friend, George Jones, the country singer," Peanutt volunteered. "I'm Linda, Charlene's younger sister, and it's nice to meet you," I said to Mr. Jones.

I then went back into the kitchen and sat down at the table with Aaron and Charlene. Peanutt and George resumed picking and singing as if they had their own little world they were playing in.

"Linda, I'd like to take you out to dinner tonight," Aaron said to me.

I told him I'd go. We stayed around the table talking to Charlene until time for dinner.

Aaron and I went to the River Bluff Restaurant to eat. We had a really good meal and a nice night out. I took a real liking to him; he was so kind and polite. After sitting and talking for a while, we decided to go back to Peanutt and Charlene's. When we got there, Peanutt and George were still picking and singing songs. They must have been writing a song too because they would sing a line, and the other one would change it. Whatever the case, they were preoccupied with what they were doing.

I was feeling a little out of place. I had never been around drinking, and I noticed that George and Peanutt both were drinking beer. Aaron had fixed himself a mixed drink and offered me one, but I told him I didn't drink. I was surprised that Charlene was letting them drink in her home. That was not like her at all. I knew she hated drinking and didn't want Peanutt to drink. I just figured it was because George was there, and she felt obligated to let them drink. Nobody was out of line, but it made me a little nervous. Charlene called me off to the side,

"Now Linda, don't worry about those men drinking, they all know how I feel about drinking, and they know I'll make them leave if they get out of line."

After that, I felt a little more at ease for I knew Charlene wasn't afraid to speak her piece if she needed to. Aaron and I were sitting on the couch beside each other. Peanutt and George finally laid the guitars down and talked to us for a while. George started out by picking on Aaron.

"Aaron, you took Linda out to dinner tonight, but you've got to leave and go back to Peoria tomorrow, and I'm gonna take her away from you as soon as you leave. I'm gonna take Linda to dinner tomorrow night."

"Oh, no Jones," Aaron replied, "I'm taking Linda with me to Peoria."

"No, you're not," George cried, "She's staying here, and you're leaving tomorrow and I ain't got nowhere to go."

George was just dying laughing and picking at Aaron. I walked off and went back to the kitchen. Aaron came in and sat down with me. Charlene and Peanutt had a really big house. It had a fully finished basement with a recreation room and a pool table. The rec room had a bar, bedroom, and a bath. Aaron asked me to go down and play a game of pool with him, and so I went. When we got to the basement, he invited me to the bedroom. I told him to forget the game of pool, and that I was going back upstairs. I went back to the kitchen.

"I thought you were going to play pool?" Charlene asked.

I told her that we decided not to. I knew I couldn't tell her what Aaron did for I knew she'd chew his rear end out, so I just kept it to myself. Aaron came back upstairs. He apologized to me over and over. I told him that if he thought I was that kind of person that he needed to forget about me. His asking me to sleep with him really offended me. Aaron asked me not to tell Charlene and Peanutt what he did, and I didn't.

Linda Jones at the George Jones Nashville Estate where George died.

George Jones' children gathering at a restaurant across from Opryland on the day of their daddy's funeral. Left to Right - Tina, Jeffrey, Charlene Montgomery, Peanutt Montgomery, Brian, Linda Jones, Georgette.

George Jones and Tammy Wynette's home on Tyne Boulevard, Nashville, Tennessee.

Goofing off.

George and Peanutt enjoying the river view.

Enjoying some good food on a cruise. Left to Right - Jody Emerson, Wild Bill Emerson, George Jones, Linda Jones, Charlene Montgomery, Peanutt Montgomery.

*Peanutt and Charlene Montgomery's mansion on
Hillsboro Road in Nashville, Tennessee.*

*Trying to figure out what to do on Memorial Day – Left to Right – Billy Robertson,
George Jones, Linda Jones, Charlene Montgomery, Peanutt Montgomery, and
Wanda Lynn Montgomery.*

*Longtime best friends - George Jones
and Country Music Recording Artist,
Tanya Tucker.*

*Teresa True Montgomery (left) and
Tina Jones hanging out.*

To: Sherman, Dr.

The Legend of George Jones

Writer: Earl Peanutt Montgomery
Publisher: Mister Magic Music, BMI
(C)&(P) APRIL 26TH 2013

IN 1931 A MOTHER GAVE BIRTH TO A SON
SHE NAMED HIM LITTLE GEORGE THE SINGER OF SONGS
IN SIX DAYS GOD MADE HEAVEN AND EARTH
THE SEVENTH DAY HE RESTED FROM HIS WORK
ON THE EIGHT DAY HE BEGIN THE LEGEND OF GEORGE JONES

IN 1956 HE BEGIN TO STRIKE IT RICH
WHY BABY WHY BECAME HIS FIRST CHARTED SONG
OPPORTUNITIES WOULD SOON ARRIVE
SINGING ON THE LOUISIANA HAYRIDE
HE KEPT ON BUILDING THE LEGEND OF GEORGE JONES

CHO.

LIKE A SUNDAY MORNING CHOIR
SONGS BEGIN TO FILL THE HOUR
SOUNDS LIKE ANGELS SINGING AROUND HEAVEN'S THRONE
THE OPRY'S NEVER BEEN THE SAME
SINCE THE ANNOUNCER SPOKE HIS NAME
LIKE WILD FIRE SPREAD THE LEGEND OF GEORGE JONES

IN TWO THOUSAND THIRTEEN COUNTRY MUSIC LOST A KING
GOD KNEW IT WAS TIME TO CALL HIM HOME
MY FRIENDS TAKE THIS FOR WHAT IT'S WORTH
HE WILL NEVER LEAVE THIS EARTH
BECAUSE HIS MUSIC LIKE HIS LEGEND LIVES ON AND ON

TAG.

LONG LIVE MY FRIEND AND THE LEGEND OF GEORGE JONES

7-30-2013

It is a honor to write this song, may God bless it always!

Earl Peanutt Montgomery

Lyrics of the original song "The Legend of George Jones" written by Earl Peanutt Montgomery and given to Dr. Sherman Smith, Publisher.

George and Linda at their Florence Hills house.

Beautiful Tammy Wynette.

I waited for a short while and told Charlene that I had to go back to our mother's. As I left, Aaron followed me to the car. He again apologized to me.

"Linda, I really do want to take you to Peoria with me," he said, "I want to marry you."

"Aaron, you don't even know me, and I don't know you any better, and there's no way I would marry you."

"Linda, I promise you that you'll never want anything the rest of your life, and I'll treat your little son as if he was my own."

"Aaron, I have just left Illinois after being there for 10 years, and I'm not about to go back there."

"Well, I own a big business in Peoria, and it's worth a whole lot of money and if you'll just wait on me, I'll sell it all and move to Alabama."

"Aaron, I can't promise you anything. I have just met you."

I told him that I really liked him, and I thought he was very nice, with the exception of the one episode, but I just didn't know him. He told me to go on to my mother's and think about it. I left and went home. I knew Aaron had to leave the next day, and I was not going back to Charlene's until he was gone. The next morning Charlene called. It was around noon.

"Linda, I want you to come over here and come now!" She yelled.

"Charlene, I'm not coming over there until Aaron leaves," I answered.

"Oh, he's already gone. I want you to take a trip with me."

"Where are we going?" I asked.

"We're going to the Bahamas, and I want you to come with us."

"Charlene, I have a child to take care of, and I can't be spending money on trips. You know I haven't got a job yet, and I just can't afford to go."

Then she told me, "George wants you to go, and he said he'd pay your way."

I told Charlene, "I don't even know George, and he doesn't

need to be paying my way to the Bahamas. It all sounds good, I really would love to go, but to let George pay my way is out of the question."

"Linda, if George didn't want you to go, he wouldn't have offered to pay your way, so come on and go, you'll have a good time. Peanutt and George both have promised not to drink on the whole trip so come on and go with us."

I could tell Charlene really did want me to go, so I asked mother to take care of Dale for me, so I could take the trip, and she agreed to watch him while I was gone. I told Charlene that I'd go, but I was not going to be obligated to anybody by going. She assured me that she had made that perfectly clear to everyone. By the time I got to Charlene's, they had already made all the arrangements. Wild Bill and Jody Emerson, a songwriting husband and wife team who were friends of Charlene, Peanutt, and George were also invited by George to go, and they accepted. It made me feel a little better because I felt like George just wanted to get a bunch of whoever to go on the trip. George had rented a motor home for us to ride in to Miami.

When we all got in the motor home to leave, Charlene, Jody, and I went to the back of the motor home to talk. Peanutt was driving, and Wild Bill and George were picking and singing. After a little while, George yelled,

"You girls come back up here!"

We all three went to the front of the motor home, and George started teasing me. "I told Aaron I was going to take his girl away and I am," George blurted out.

I thought, *"Oh Lord, what does he mean?"* Charlene just laughed it off, but I could tell George was serious about me.

George didn't drink a drop of alcohol. We all laughed, talked, picked, and sang songs the whole trip. We got nearly halfway to Miami, and the air conditioner went out on the motor home. It began to get very very hot. We all thought we'd smother to death in that thing. To make things worse, Wild Bill and Jody decided to go to bed, so they'd feel good the next day. George, Charlene, and I continued to sit up front and talk to Peanutt while he drove. About five minutes after Jody and Wild Bill had gone to bed, we smelled this terrible odor in the motor home.

We all three looked at each other and George said, "What in the world is that?" Of course Charlene didn't know and neither did I.

"Maybe Peanutt ran over a dead dog," Charlene commented.

"No, I haven't," Peanutt exclaimed.

George yelled out to Wild Bill, "What's that odor I smell?"

Jody yelled back. "George, it's Wild Bill's feet. They always smell like that if he wears tennis shoes."

"Good Lord!" George yelled again. "Tell him to wash his feet!"

"George, it won't do any good, they just smell that way," Jody yelled back.

"Well, tell him to put his shoes back on and sleep in them if he has to. We can't stand that odor!"

There was no circulating air in the motor home at all, only the smell of rotten feet. I thought I'd die. Finally, Peanutt pulled into a place for us to sleep. We all went to bed on couches, and anywhere we could make a bed and sleep the rest of the night. We drove on in to Miami the next day and boarded the Flavia. We were on our way to Freeport, Bahamas. It was so exciting, but we knew when the trip was over it would be rough going home with no air in the motor home. The cruise was great. Nobody drank at all. We just had a very good time playing some games on the ship, shopping during the day, and finding different places to eat during the evening. I think I gained five pounds in that one week.

George bought all three of us girls a white cap with ribbons and golf tees. I still have mine. When we first got back to the ship, Peanutt, George, and Wild Bill decided to go to the casino. Charlene, Jody, and I wanted to get some sun, so we put on our bikinis and went out to sun bathe. We climbed to the very top of the ship to lie in the sun. It was the Captain's deck. Charlene had been there before and told us it was a private deck, and we were not supposed to be up there. It didn't turn out to be too private after all. One of the Captains walked up to the deck and started talking to us. He was a tall, dark, and handsome young man. He thought he'd flirt with us a little bit. I kept watching the area where the steps were to the top of the deck. I was afraid Peanutt, George, and Wild Bill might come up there and find that guy there, and I knew George would not like it. Neither would Peanutt, but the guy just kept laughing and talking to us. I hadn't paid much attention to him until he reached down and pinched me on the cheek and said,

"I can tell you are Italian."

I pushed back from him and my lounge chair turned over. About that time the ship whistle blew, and it sounded like it was right in our ears. The unexpected loud noise scared me half to death, so I screamed. The Captain started laughing and went over to help me up.

"I'm sorry I didn't mean to scare you," he said. I thanked him for his help.

"I think we need to go back down to our rooms and get dressed up and go find the guys," I told Charlene and Jody, and they both agreed.

"Don't let me run you off!" The Captain yelled as we fled the scene.

"Linda, George would have had a fit if he'd seen that guy talking to you," Jody said while we were walking to our rooms.

"I know, that's why I wanted to get out of there," I answered.

"Peanutt wouldn't have liked it any more than George," Charlene added. "I was hoping he'd get out from up there and leave us alone."

Jody, Charlene, and I laughed about it later. We went to our rooms, dressed, and went looking for Peanutt, George, and Wild Bill. We found them playing the slot machines in the casino. George looked at me and asked, "Did you get enough sun?"

"Yeah, we got a little, but we didn't stay out too long," I answered.

About that time, crazy Charlene spoke up, "Yeah, she got quite a bit, even the Captain said he could tell she was Italian because she was so dark and he pinched her on the cheek."

"What the hell was he doing pinching you on the cheek?" George asked.

"Oh, George, he was just trying to make us feel good," I replied.

"If I'd seen that little wimp touching you, he'd think feel good, he'd feel good alright, real good when I got through with him," George said.

Wild Bill changed the subject. "Hey, let's go get something to eat, I'm starving."

Everybody must have been starving because they all agreed to go eat. At least, it got George's mind off of the Captain. Everyone stayed straight on the whole trip until the night of the Captain's dinner. That night, George decided to have a drink. I think he thought we might run into the Captain who pinched me on the cheek and maybe if he got high, he'd wiggle his way out of going. It was to be the big night for partying on the ship, but we missed it. It was on this trip that I realized that George was a good man. I really liked him, and I knew that he liked me as well.

When George and I got back to Peanutt and Charlene's house in Florence, we decided we would call it a relationship. The relationship never ended. We stayed with Peanutt and Charlene until we could get a place of our own. The breakup between George and Tammy didn't look promising on them ever getting back together, so George was beginning to feel it was time for us to go forward with our lives. He finally bought us a little house on Wright Drive about two blocks from where Peanutt and Charlene lived. George called Billy Wilhite, his booker and road manager, and asked him to move to Florence. George told Billy that there was a brand new house for sale next door to us, and George wanted Billy and his wife Rose to buy it.

Billy and Rose came to Florence and looked at the house.

They really liked it and bought it. Billy and Rose moved in almost a month later. We all pitched in and helped them get situated. Rose became a close friend to all of us. We had lots of fun doing things together. We'd take trips to Florida for a week at a time. We'd go camping out with Billy, Rose, Charlene, Peanutt, Wild Bill, and his wife Jody. We just simply had fun. George wasn't drinking hardly at all. Peanutt wasn't drinking at this time. Of course, Billy didn't drink, and neither did any of us women. We would travel with George when he had a show to do. George wanted Peanutt, Charlene, and me to go everywhere he went. It was a happy time for all of us.

Billy and George would occasionally have to go to Nashville. George would always call me and tell me what he wanted for supper. He'd tell me when he'd be home, and he'd always do exactly what he said he'd do. After we all got settled into our new places, George wanted me to get my son Dale to come live with us. He had been staying with my mother while we were gone. I'd go see him every day or two and spend a few hours with him, but this was bothering me. I needed Dale with me, and he needed me. He lived with George and me the entire time we were together but would go stay with mother if we had to be out of town.

George realized that we needed to do something special with Dale, so we took Dale and his friend, Marty Robertson, Marty's parents, Billy and Barbara Robertson, Peanutt, Charlene, and their daughter, Theresa True, to Panama City Beach for a week. Everybody stayed straight and had a good time. It was a get together for all three families.

Once back at home, George returned to playing his show dates, I was going with him most of the time. I enjoyed going with him and watching his shows. He was hardly ever drinking a beer. He was so happy. He was enjoying doing his dates.

There was never a dull minute around George. He was full of energy and was always making plans to do something. It was either a trip to the Bahamas, Florida, camping out, or looking at houses. He was so much fun to be with.

We were out riding in a subdivision one day, and a man was standing out in front of his house and leaning up against his pickup truck. George stopped, rolled his window down, and asked the guy if the house was for sale.

"'NO!' The man said loudly. "This is where I live, but I can build you a house. I'm D. G. Lovell, and I'm a builder."

"Do you have any lots?" George asked Mr. Lovell.

He told George that he had a really nice lot on a lake at Brooks Acres. George asked if he could see the lot and D. G. Lovell said he could take him out there right then, so we followed him out to see the property.

George loved the lot and told D.G. that he wanted to buy it and wanted him to build us an A-frame house on it. George and D.G. worked out a deal for the lot and the house. Meanwhile, we all got a good job out of the deal. The lot had to be cleared, and George told D.G. that he would clear it himself. George, Peanutt, Charlene, Billy, Rose, and I cleared that big lake lot by ourselves. We worked as hard as we could to get it ready for the builder. It was a big job. Everyone of us broke out with poison oak. Billy looked pitiful. He was fair-skinned, and he had red rashes all over him. He had to walk with his legs apart to keep them from rubbing against the blisters. George would bust out laughing every time he saw Billy. Billy had put cala-mine lotion all over him. Peanutt, Charlene, and I began to itch all over. We also broke out in blisters. It tickled George to death; he didn't have one blister on him. The worse part of that ordeal was we had to go back the next day and continue working to clear the property.

The next day while we were working, George picked up a leaf of poison oak, put it in his mouth, and chewed it up. Char-lene had a fit. She told George eating that stuff would kill him. He laughed at her and told her he was not allergic to it, and he wouldn't have a single blister. And he didn't. We all wound up having to go to the doctor but George wasn't bothered at all.

We finally got the lot cleared and ready to build on. D. G. began building the A-frame. It was a cozy lake house, and we really enjoyed it. There was a big deck over the lake, and we'd spend a lot of time down there fishing and cooking out. All our friends would come over and fish off the deck. Peanutt and Charlene were always around, and so were Billy and Rose Wilhite.

George had a niece named Mary Nell. She was trying to get into the music business as a singer. She came to live with George and me. I really liked her, and she was so much fun to live with. A little later on, her mother, Doris, who was George's sister, came and spent two weeks with us. She too was a sweet lady but was a little reserved. After Doris left, then Ruth, George's other sister, came and spent time with us. Unlike Doris, Ruth was not at all reserved. She voiced her opinion on everything and was quick to do so. Ruth talked all the time. George told Charlene before Ruth ever got to our house that she was fixing to meet somebody who could out talk her. Charlene doubted that.

Ruth came and on the first night of her visit, she found out that Charlene was an Aries. Ruth was an Aries too, and that seemed important to her. Ruth stayed up after everybody except Charlene had gone to bed. Charlene hated to tell her that she needed to go to bed, so she sat up and listened to Ruth talk. Charlene hardly had a chance to say a word. Then Charlene finally went to bed at 4:00 a.m. The next morning Ruth told George,

"This damn gal kept me up all night."

George just died laughing. He knew what had happened. He looked at Charlene and asked if she had a chance to say much? Charlene only smiled at him. Ruth stayed for a week or so and then went back to Texas.

We had lived at the lake house in Brooks Acres just outside of Florence in a little town called Killen, Alabama for about a year. George began to drink a little, but not bad. He'd go into Nashville and when he'd come home, he'd be drinking, but his drinking never really got out of hand. George made Mary Nell nervous when he was drinking. Finally, Mary Nell thought George might be tired of her living there, so she moved to Texas.

George became restless. He went looking and found a big three-story house at Kendale Gardens in Florence. It was a little closer to town and to where Peanutt and Charlene lived. The people who lived in the house wanted a place on the lake. So, it worked out to where George would sell the people his lake house, and George would buy their house. This worked out really well for both families. We got the house George wanted, and the people moved into the lake house on five acres.

We moved into Kendale Gardens. We were not there long until George had found a new manager. His name was Alsey "Shug" Baggott. Billy and Rose sold their house and moved back to Toccoa, Georgia. Shug was the new man in on the scene. This decision was the beginning of the worst time of my life and almost the ending of George's.

George and I had a wonderful life together. We never argued about anything and got along perfectly. We really loved each other and were very happy. I never had anybody be as good to me as George was. He always treated me with respect and had carried me places with him to do his show dates. We laughed, talked, planned things together and really enjoyed life. He'd give me a little money to spend, bought me beautiful jewelry, kept me in a nice car, and was very much a gentleman with me. I loved George, and I wanted him to have the freedom he needed. I never complained about him having to be gone on his trips to Nashville. I just took care of the house and cooked whatever he wanted and made sure things got done while he was away on his trips.

George planted a big garden after we moved in the house at Kendale Gardens. Peanutt, Charlene, and I helped him get it all set out. He bought a couple of horses from Melba Montgomery and her husband, Jack Solomon. We were going to ride horses and enjoy our new house and five acres. We had lived there for almost two months when Dewayne Phillips, Dale Phillips, and their dad, Buddy Phillips, moved from Texas and came to live with us. George thought that they could be a lot of help around the house and could keep the five acres mowed and maintain the pool. That worked out just fine for a while, but George was already involved with this Shug guy and instead of things getting better, they actually started falling apart.

I tried to make life a little better for George. I called Tammy Wynette and asked her to let Georgette come and spend some time with George. Tammy agreed to let her come. I also called Shirley Corley, George's wife before Tammy, and asked for Brian and Jeff to come stay for a while with us. She agreed to let them come. They all three came to visit at the same time. I thought it would not only be good for George but would be good for the kids. Georgette had not been around her brothers, and I thought it would give them some time to get to know each other a little better. George was tickled to death when he came home and found out he had three of his four children there. I would love for Susan to have been there too, but she was already married and was living in Ardmore, Alabama. George had been around Susan quite a bit. She had married Herman Smith and had lived in Nashville, and George and Tammy had hired Herman to do a lot of work for them. George had seen a lot of Susan recently but had not had a lot of time with Georgette and the boys since his divorce from Tammy.

After all the kids went back to their homes, the Phillips family decided to move back to Texas. They knew George was not the same as he had always been. None of us knew exactly what was happening, but we knew there was definitely something strange going on. Peanutt and Charlene had begun to wonder what was troubling George? He was not the person they had always known. Strange things started happening around him. His bus driver, Jimmy Guyton, disappeared. Nobody knew what happened to him, including his wife or kids, and is still missing to this day. Snakes started showing up on our doorstep, people were following me, I started getting strange phone calls, and then it became worse; there were threatening phone calls.

"You better get away from George, or you're gonna die," or *"If you love your son, you'll leave George."*

These are examples of the many calls that were coming in nearly every day. Shug offered me twenty-thousand dollars to leave George. I told him that I wasn't with George for the money, and that I wouldn't leave him. I knew where the calls were coming from. It had to do with someone around the people George was involved with. Peanutt and Charlene were receiving the same types of calls. They were threatened all the time. Someone would call in the early morning hours, and they'd say "stay away from George if you want to live." Then they'd tell Peanutt and Charlene, "If you tell George about this call, you'll be sorry."

Peanutt and Charlene were visiting us one night, and Peanutt told me about the calls. He was upset.

"I was warned not to tell George about the calls, and I guess I better not say anything to him about it, but I'm tired of it."

Peanutt had a couple of beers. "Charlene I've got to leave, and I've got to leave right now."

"Okay, Peanutt, we'll go when you're ready," Charlene replied.

Charlene told me she'd call me later. They left. On the way home, Peanutt picked up the four beers that were left in his six-pack and threw them out the car window.

"Charlene," He said. "I'm quitting right now."

Charlene called me and told me what had happened after they left. She said they had gone to our brother-in-law's house, who was a preacher, and Peanutt wanted to talk to him. She said James Lee, the preacher, and Peanutt went for a ride. Charlene stayed with our other sister, Nell Lee (the preacher's wife), while Peanutt was gone. When Peanutt and James came back, Charlene said she didn't ask any questions; they just got in the car and went home.

That night Peanutt tossed and turned and couldn't sleep. She said he was so restless, and she didn't know what was going on with him. The next morning, she said Peanutt wanted to go see Irene Green, who was our mother. Mother was a Christian lady, and Peanutt wanted to talk to her. Charlene said when Peanutt came back to the car after his visit with Mother, he told her that he had just become a Christian, and he felt like he had just had a ton of weight lifted off of his chest. Charlene wasn't sure about his commitment to the Lord but figured time would tell.

George was one of the first people Peanutt had to tell about his soul saving, life-changing experience. George wasn't sure what to think about this change in his good friend. George hardly understood what was going on with Peanutt. He began to question if Peanutt was sincere or not. George soon realized Peanutt meant business about his commitment to the Lord. Peanutt would no longer drink with George. He refused to go on the road with George if he was working in a club. He would not run with George if George was drinking. Peanutt quit everything that he felt would not be pleasing to the Lord. He even quit writing country songs if they had to do with promoting sex, divorce, alcohol, clubbing, and such things that he felt would promote sin.

Things began to get rough around George. It was becoming pure hell. I think Peanutt had seen what was happening to George and saw what that kind of life leads to, and he wanted to get away from the whole thing. George became upset with Peanutt. He thought Peanutt had turned his back on him even though that wasn't the case. George didn't know about all the life-threatening calls we were receiving. We couldn't tell him. Even our telephone lines were tapped. Charlene and I would make calls to certain people and say things that we knew would get around if we put out information that would upset them. We'd make plans with certain friends to say things that we knew would travel like wild fire. We wanted to make sure the lines were tapped, and they were. When the gossip started, we knew then what had happened. They had to hear the conversations on the phone to even know it was all a set up to find out about the phone lines. It wasn't a very good plan, but it got us what we wanted to know.

"Linda, if the phone is tapped, you'll know in no more than a couple of days," Charlene said. "I've said some things that they would love to hear, and they'll run with it. You wait and see."

Sure enough, she was right. We did similar things to find out who was following us. We'd show up at places that we weren't supposed to be, and we knew that we were being followed. What we didn't know was who was following us, and who had put someone up to it. Finally, it all came to a head. We found out the answer to the whole puzzle. The culprits were the people who wanted control of George. They had already offered me money to leave him, and when I refused, they thought they'd scare me away. That didn't work either.

The life George and I once had was gone. It was over. I knew I couldn't handle him on cocaine. Drinking was bad enough, but cocaine was out of the question. I stayed with him, but for the last three years it was pure hell. I was not a person to put on the dog (as the old saying goes). I was Linda, and I was true to myself. I knew how to dress, and I knew how to act around people, but I didn't exalt myself just because George was a legend. I didn't care about the fame thing. I loved George because of the man he was, not the star he was. It was hard not to love George. He was a very good-hearted man. He was good to everybody. He was kind, sharing, loving, and compassionate. He'd help anybody if the person needed help. He was nice to our neighbors, and we had loads of good friends.

After we found out that George was on cocaine, then we knew what had happened to him. We also understood the phone calls, the tapped phone lines, the stalkers, and the threats. It was the people in the drug ring. We knew it was a serious situation. It was big money and power and control and much bigger than we needed to mess with. When you're messing up plans for someone whose counting on six figures or more in profits, you'd better take heed to the threats. We know that people would kill for a lot less.

George was consumed. It was too late to try and do anything. They had brainwashed him. They had total control, and they had him in debt to them. They used him in every way they could to gain a dollar. Big deals were being made in George's name. With almost every one of them falling through, and mostly after his front money had been paid, it actually got to the dangerous point.

The last three years for George and me were turbulent most of the time. Throughout 1978-1980 and parts of 1981, George was on cocaine and heavily drinking. He couldn't stay in one place over an hour or so. He would jump in his car and drive around for hours at a time. We'd head out to Nashville, and the whole time he'd be screaming in an outrage about who he was going kill when they got there, and how he was going do it. He'd get right in my face, pulling at me while I was trying to drive and swearing that he was going to kill them all for taking advantage of him. I'd try to push him away, so I could see how to drive. I was afraid he was going to cause me to have a bad wreck, but he wouldn't listen to me. He was mad at Shug for one, but there were others he was threatening as well. He knew Shug had messed his life up. George knew that. I actually could understand why George was so furious with Shug, but I knew he didn't need to kill anybody.

I tried to get George to forget it all and to get away from Shug.

"I can't get away. They'll kill me if I don't kill them first!" George would always say.

George knew a whole lot more than I knew about the situation. He had bad checks floating all over the place. He thought he had money in the bank, but checks for large sums had been written out, and George had no idea what they had been written for. His bank account was constantly on overdraft. It got so badly out of hand that George finally got into a financial bind and had to file bankruptcy, which he did not want to do. He had no choice. He had been robbed by so-called managers and drug dealers. George became so discouraged that he began missing more and more show dates which led to more stress for him because of the threats of lawsuits for not showing up for the performances.

Many times George and I would head out for Texas or Florida, wherever his show dates were with all good intentions of him making his dates, but somewhere along the way he'd become paranoid, and then would imagine someone was following us. He'd make us take a side road saying we had to lose them. I'd try to explain to him that we needed to keep going, so he'd make his date. When I refused to comply with what he wanted, he'd get mad, grab the steering wheel, and pull at it telling me to "get off of the damn road." He'd scream at me and demand that I take a side road and lose them; so finally I'd exit somewhere and drive away from the main drag.

We'd ride for hours down winding roads, and we didn't have any idea where we'd wind up? Once George felt safe, he would be fine. I would be completely worn out from driving for hours, listening to him, and wrestling with him to leave the steering wheel alone. Many times I'd drive for two days with no rest at all. My head would actually be throbbing from a headache, but we were so far from home, and no one to help me drive. George was all messed up, and I certainly wasn't going to ride with him behind the wheel.

I had to handle these difficult circumstances alone. When George did actually make a show, Shug and his gang of thugs would meet us there. They were all shined up in their expensive suits, every white hair in place, and looked like they were the stars after I had been through pure hell trying to get George to the show date. They would make derogatory remarks about my appearance.

Sometimes I didn't have a chance to change clothes after wearing the same outfit for a couple of days or more or get my hair fixed. I had no choice but to appear the way I arrived. It had never been that way before Shug came into the picture. I always had plenty of time to get ready to go to shows. I always looked nice, but Shug wanted me to look haggard, worn, and nasty. He wanted George to notice how out of sorts I was becoming and use that against me to get me out of the way. He wanted Peanutt and Charlene gone no matter what the cost. The sad part of all this was he would get what he wanted.

After we had gone on one long trip that felt like it was never going to end, I told George that after we got home that he had to go get help to get off drugs, or I was going to leave him. I told him I was no longer going to take abuse. He agreed to go to Eliza Coffee Memorial Hospital in Florence to get help. I made arrangements and had him committed. He said he felt he could get off of drugs with the help of the hospital. He promised me he'd try his best to straighten out his life and get our lives back together. He was serious, and I knew he was a sick man who needed help, but I was afraid of what that bunch of drug dealers in Nashville would try and do once he got out of the hospital.

I told George I was willing to stick it out with him because I loved him and wanted him to get his life back. I also told him I expected him to do his part and to try and help himself for his own sake. I stayed at the hospital day and night with him. I'd take my baths right there in his room. I'd have Charlene bring me a change of clothes and take my dirty ones with her every day. George didn't want me to leave him, not for a minute, and I didn't. Each day he was showing a little more strength.

"When I get out of here, you'll see a change. I promise you Linda, I'll straighten up if you'll not leave me." George was broken and sincere.

I didn't have any intentions of leaving George; he needed me and I wasn't about to abandon him in his time of need, but I couldn't let him know that.

When he was finally released from the hospital and we returned home, George was doing fine. He was off of cocaine and wasn't drinking much either. George was staying away from Shug now, and his cronies couldn't stand it. George stayed straight for three months. During this time, we had moved to Knightsbridge Road in the Creekwood subdivision in Florence.

George's son, Jeffrey, had married, and he and his wife, Sue, had come to live with us. Sue was such a sweet girl. She was so easy going and just a lovely little lady. I just loved her to death (I still talk to her today occasionally). Jeffrey got a job, and Sue was with me when George had to go out of town.

George was doing better than he had been for a long time. He loved our house, and it was only a few streets from where Peanutt and Charlene lived. We were always doing little things together. George was happy that Jeffrey and Sue were there. He really loved Sue like his own daughter.

The vampires in Nashville weren't happy that things were going so well in George's life. They reminded me of a bunch of buzzards sitting back waiting for a chance to grab their prey. I tried to keep things from George that I knew would upset him, but they made sure that he heard about everything. They'd tell him about the stories reported in the magazines, so he would buy them and read about himself. The tabloids would say things like, *"George Jones is reportedly sick, battle worn, sleeping in his car cause he has no place to live, and no place to go."*

George would get all bent out of shape about what he read because the stories were nothing but lies. George was doing very well. He had a brand new house. He always had a home. George was never without a place to go, he never slept in his car, and I was at the door to greet him every time he came home.

Even if the story about George not having a place to call his own, and nowhere to go, had been true, he had loyal and true friends who looked out for him. He knew he could always call and count on Peanutt and Charlene. They would never turn George away under any circumstances. George knew that. Peanutt and Charlene both loved George. They would have died for that man. They did everything they could to help him, but that bunch of heathens in Nashville despised them for lending George a helping hand. They wanted to force George to return to them for help.

George was strong enough to make it for about a year. He had been doing his show dates. We were doing well together and happy. Life was treating us good. He was paying for our new home, and we had Jeffrey and Sue with us. Peanutt and Charlene were going to the show dates with us again, and life had returned to normal.

In early 1979, all hell broke loose again. Shug came back into the picture. This time he was determined to bring George to the bottom. George would go for days without eating. He snorted cocaine heavier than ever. Sue and Jeffrey returned to Texas, and things were getting really bad.

George became paranoid and confused. He'd come home completely wiped out. I'd sit on the side of the bed and feed him broth and chicken soups trying to get him to gain some strength. He'd refuse to eat anything, but I could get him to sip beef broth through a straw. He was losing weight and looked like he was about to die. It was so scary seeing him waste away. I knew George had to have some help. I didn't know what on earth to do, and I knew I couldn't overpower the cocaine addiction or the people who supplied it.

George's weight dropped to 97 pounds. I begged him to get help, but he refused. I sat beside him night after night trying to get him to eat, but all he wanted was Jack Daniels, 7-up, and his cocaine. His colon was completely gone, and I'd watch him fall off to sleep and wonder if he'd ever wake up. I finally called Peanutt.

"Peanutt, if George don't get some help he is going to die," I said. "Peanutt, if you love George, you'll get him some help."

"I will try my best to get him into Hillcrest Hospital in Birmingham," Peanutt replied. "I'm not sure what I'll have to do, but I'm gonna do whatever it takes."

Peanutt knew George was dying. He had been out to eat with George and saw George eating chicken off his plate with his teeth and shaking his head until it fell off the bone. Peanutt knew George would never do something like that if he was in his right mind. Peanutt had seen George's strange behavior firsthand and knew something had to be done right away.

Peanutt went to Judge Duncan and got George's Power of Attorney, so he could have him committed to the hospital. Peanutt called me that same day,

"Linda, George will be picked up by the Sheriff and will be admitted to Hillcrest Hospital in Birmingham. I have already set it up. George will be mad at me, but I'd rather have him mad at me than for me to see him dead."

"You are right, Peanutt, George has got to have help." I was so proud of what Peanutt had done.

George was picked up and carried to Hillcrest Hospital by a Court Order. Sure, it made George furious at first, but once he got settled, and Dr. Knuckles told him that he would not have lived another thirty days if he had not gotten help, George began to realize that what Peanutt had done was strictly to save his life. George was no longer furious at Peanutt, but appreciated and loved him for it.

I get sick to my stomach when I read in other books that have been written where everybody else tries to take credit for being George's mentors, friends, and an influence over him during these dark places in his life.

After George was well, he was back on the road. He was moving away from me very quickly, and I was helpless to stop what he was doing. He was drinking heavily and was being influenced by some very bad women. A couple of these people were hanging on to George and trying to get him to take them on some of his trips.

On one particular occasion, George was drunk and asked the women to go to New York with him to see him perform in a concert. They all went together. George got tired of them very quickly and then came home to me but left them in New York. He went to bed to get some rest. The phone rang. I answered, and there was a woman on the line asking to speak to George. I told her he was asleep, and that I would not wake him up. I asked who she was, and she said Nancy.

"He left my ass in New York, and I want to talk to him!" She yelled.

I hung up on her. About an hour later, a man called and told me that the Mafia was on their way down from Nashville to come run houses and if I ever listened to anyone in my life, I had better listen to what he had to say.

"You had better get out of that house and get out now, or you could be hurt bad," The man explained.

Dale was there, so I finally decided to take him to my mother's, which was only about three miles away. When I made it to my mother's, I decided to call my house. Some man answered and then handed the phone to the woman who said her name was Nancy. I told her that I would be home in a few minutes, and she had better be out of my house when I got there.

I went home, she was gone, the man was gone, and so was George. Finally, Billy Danley (a friend of George) called me.

"Linda, George wanted me to call and tell you that he is with me. He wanted me to hide him from that bunch that took him off from home. He said he had to get away from them. I've got him with me. George said that he'd get in touch with you as soon as he could."

I was fighting mad. I called Charlene and told her what was going on. She was highly upset with George. George then went to Peanutt and Charlene's and had Charlene call his house to see if anybody would answer? Nancy answered the phone. She had gone into my home and would not leave. George asked Charlene to call his house and tell the woman to get out, but she refused to leave.

George continued to stay with Peanutt and Charlene hoping the squatting woman would get out of our house. Finally, he sent Jimmy and Ann Hills (his booking agent) over there to try and persuade her to leave. Nancy decided to overdose on pills. Jimmy had to rush her to the hospital to have her stomach pumped. Unbelievably, they decided to bring her back to our house to recover. When George became aware of the situation, he started calling her and cursing her out, trying to get her to leave.

"Get out of my house you whore, you bitch, do you hear me? Get out of my damn house."

George would scream at her on the phone, Nancy would not budge. I could have called the police and had her removed, but I was afraid everything would wind up in the news. I knew George didn't need that, so I backed off and left it up to George to get her out.

A few days later, she overdosed again. She had to call Jimmy Hills to take her back to the hospital and have her stomach pumped again. This went on for days, and then turned into weeks, and finally I told George that I was not going to put up with this mess any longer. George begged me to come over to Peanutt's, but I would not. I was mad at him for getting himself into such a bad situation.

Charlene told George that she didn't want me to come back to him. George reacted and was angry enough that he went home with the intentions of removing Nancy from the house. He was physically going to carry her back to Louisiana. When George headed the car toward Louisiana, Nancy realized what he was doing. She suddenly jumped from the car and broke her arm when she hit the pavement.

George had to take her to the hospital to get her arm set and in a cast. Finally, I told George that I would not come home until Nancy was completely out of our home and lives. Nancy took up residence in my home with all my possessions still in the house and would not leave. George had to go home. He was in a bad situation he couldn't get out of.

Nancy invited some of her friends over to our house to party for a few days. George called Peanutt and Charlene and asked them to come over to the house. When they arrived at the house, Charlene said there were men and women there that she didn't know, so she left.

George finally realized that I was not coming home. I had to find a place to live, so I rented an apartment. I did stay at my mother's place as a safety matter until George and Nancy moved on. Nancy moved her children into our home with her and enrolled them in school. One of the girls didn't stay and went back home to live with her father.

An incident occurred when Peanutt and Charlene were visiting at George's house while Nancy was there. Nancy was spouting off to Charlene and irritating her. They were getting into a pretty heated discussion when Peanutt broke it up by taking Charlene home. Peanutt did the right thing because Charlene has a temper and if you push her to that point, she'll level with you in a heartbeat and never blink an eye.

George and Nancy were finally together. George had no other choice. He was stuck with what he had gotten himself into, but he'd still call Charlene from time to time trying to get me to come home to him, but I wasn't about to get myself into that mess. Eventually they moved to Louisiana for a while and then wound up in Texas. When they founded and built an amusement park, George decided he would cave in and marry Nancy. The date was March 5, 1983. During the entire time he was with Nancy, George would call me and ask me to come back to him. I always refused.

George's sister, Ruth, and her husband, Buster, came to my house one day and told me that they were with George at the Wheeler Lodge, and that George had sent them after me to come up there and see him. I told Ruth to tell him that I would not stoop that low. I knew he was a married man, or at least I thought he was, and that I would not meet him as long as he was with Nancy. I knew that I had never gotten a divorce from George and was still his common-law wife, but that still didn't make it okay with me. He was living with another woman, and I would not do to her what she did to me.

There have been occasions throughout the years that George would call me and talk to me, but I have never agreed to see him in person alone. There were people around George that kept me informed about him. They knew how I felt about George and thought they were doing me a favor by telling me things, but I really wasn't interested anymore. I knew that there was a picture being painted to the public that everything was fine and dandy. It was said that George had completely quit drinking and hadn't had a drop of alcohol in such a long time. I knew better than that. I knew what was going on, but the real truth came out when he wrecked his car by hitting a bridge that nearly killed him. He was intoxicated that day. So you can paint all the pictures you want, but the truth will come out.

I know that George was not as good to Nancy as everybody was being told he was. I also knew that she had to go through a lot of hell before it ever got to where it was in his older years. Everybody wants to give someone else credit for George getting straightened out, but what really straightened George out was his age and his health. I like to give credit to George for coming to his senses and realizing that he either had to straighten up or die.

Peanutt Montgomery was the one who saved his life a long time ago by putting him in the hospital in Hillcrest. George would have died back there if Peanutt hadn't put him in Hillcrest. Dr. Knuckles told George he would not have lived another thirty days if he hadn't been admitted to the hospital. I'm thankful that things settled down for him and Nancy. I think she has been good for him, especially in his later years. He had to have somebody to take care of him, and I think she did a good job. I also think George finally started depending on her, and she hung in there with him through thick and thin, and I know she stuck it out with him right to the end. She highly resented Peanutt and Charlene and would not let George have any connection to them, but she didn't know how much Charlene and Peanutt had tried to help George.

I'm thankful that George did apologize to Peanutt and asked his forgiveness before he died. George didn't have to go to that trouble. Peanutt was never mad at George about anything. They didn't have anything against Nancy except the fact that she wouldn't let them have any association with George.

In 1986, I wanted to get remarried, but the judge pointed her finger at me and said, "You won't be marrying anybody until you get a divorce from George Jones." I told her that George was already remarried, so what did it matter. She said he might think he's married, but he's not, and don't you ever think that two wrongs make a right. I asked the judge what I should do? She plainly said go get a lawyer and file for a divorce. I went to a lawyer and explained what I needed to do. He wanted me to hit George for a lot of money.

"No. I only want enough to pay my legal bills and nothing else," I said.

"No, you deserve and have a right to some of this money," he explained.

When I went down to sign the divorce papers, my Attorney took one-third of the money and gave me the rest. I had to sign a bunch of papers, and then he told me I was now divorced and free to get married.

That was the end of my relationship with George Jones. I felt better now that the divorce was over. I went on with my life. I loved George, and I still love him and will always love him. He was very good to me, and I'll never forget it. He died knowing that as well as I do.

I think George really cared for Nancy toward the end of his life. I think she had to be a tough lady to be able to stay with him; especially, when he was on cocaine so badly. Once he had totally settled down, I hope there are no hard feelings for either of them. I just wanted to set the record straight. I am his fourth wife and feel that I should be recognized for that.

....

CHAPTER FIFTEEN

The Truth Shall Prevail

Proverbs 22:1-2: *"A good name is rather to be chosen than great riches, and loving favor rather than silver and gold. The rich and the poor meet together: the Lord is the maker of them all."*

George is worthy of a good name rather than the bad ones he has obtained by the rowdy life style of his early years in the music business. He is a man who has always entertained the poor as well as the rich. I'm not speaking of entertaining them with his talents but through the goodness of his heart. He enjoyed going to different people's homes and just sitting around talking and laughing with the people he liked. He liked poor people. For one thing, George felt most comfortable around people who were down to earth. He could relax and be himself, and I think it made him realize how blessed he truly was.

George liked people who were real and not fakes. He never cared for people who were always putting on a "show." If a person seemed to be too uppity-uppity, George would sometimes find a way to bring them down a notch or two. He never exalted himself above other people even though he knew he was a legend. In all my years with George Jones, I never knew him to be any other way. Misunderstood? He was most definitely. Down to earth? One of the most humble people you could ever meet.

George's attitude toward mankind was different from most people of his caliber. He cared for people in a different way than you might expect. Sometimes he reminded me of the Scripture in Proverbs 14:31, *"He that oppresseth the poor reproacheth his Maker; but he that honoureth him hath mercy on the poor."* George felt a lot of mercy for people and such feelings have to come from God. George most likely was never aware of his goodness.

In the eyes of some people, it was not good for George to associate or spend time with people who were not on his financial level. I totally disagree with that way of thinking.

Proverbs 14:12, *"There is a way which seemeth right unto a man, but the end thereof are the ways of death."*

George lived a long time for some reason, and I truly believe it was because he had been good to people who were less fortunate than he was. He had feelings for those people, and his feelings were real; he was not phony with them. I feel that God blesses a person for the good deeds they do whether they are rich or poor.

Proverbs 16:9, *"A man's heart devises his way; but the Lord directs his path."*

I believe the Lord had a hand in many things George did. I think he led him in a lot of the paths he took in life and led him out of some as well. It's always good for a person to be nice to those we don't even know. The Bible says in Hebrews 13:2 that when we are kind to strangers, we may have entertained angels and have not been aware of it. George had a natural innate ability to know how to treat people fairly. The kindnesses he showed to people could have been a lesson he learned from the hard knocks during his childhood days. There is absolutely nothing wrong with being rich and famous, but there is something wrong with exalting yourself above other people who are not as fortunate as you.

Just like the Bible says in James 2:2-10:

"For if there come unto your assembly a man with a gold ring, in goodly apparel, and there come in also a poor man in vile raiment; and you have respect to him that wears the gay clothing and say unto him, Sit thou here in a good place; and say to the poor, Stand thou there, or sit under my footstool; are you not then partial in your-

selves, and are become judges of evil thoughts? Hearken, my beloved children, hath not God chosen the poor of this world rich in faith, and heirs of the kingdom which he hath promised to them that love him? But you have despised the poor. Do not rich men oppress you, and draw you before the judgment seats? Do not they blaspheme that worthy name by the which you are called? If you fulfill the royal law according to scripture, Thou shalt love thy neighbor as thyself, you will do well. But if you have respect to persons you commit sin, and are convinced of the law as transgressors. For whosoever shall keep the whole law, and yet offend in one point, he is guilty of all."

Of course there were circumstances in George's life that would prevent him from being able to be friendly to everybody he met, but I'm speaking of times that were permissible for him to be kind and nice to people that were less fortunate or poor. It was just a natural thing with George. I believe those qualities came from the good spirit in him, and good spirits certainly don't come from the Devil. The point I am driving home is that George was never a mean person. He was never the bad guy some folks would have you believe. George Jones had a heart of gold.

He was never high-minded and was always compassionate with those people he met whom he felt needed it. God truly blessed George in many ways. He gave him talent, fortune, fame, health, a great family, and a long life. I am not trying to make a Saint out of George, nor am I trying to say that he's never done anything wrong. What I am defending is the fact that George was a much better person than the picture a lot of people have painted of him. He was much more of a man than he has been given credit for. Just because the tabloids print something about a person doesn't make it true. A ton of information was printed about George Jones that was not only untrue but complete nonsense. They never knew the man.

Proverbs 19:17 says, *"He that hath pity upon the poor lends to the Lord, and that which he has given will he pay him again."*

I believe the Lord has repaid George many times. I think about the times that George's career was declining and wondered if he could ever recover and get back to the top. Before I could even blink, George had another hit record. This is just proof that God does what he says he will do.

"Whoso stops his ears at the cry of the poor, he also shall cry himself, but shall not be heard." Proverbs 21:13.

George had a bad wreck, which caused a near death experience, and I believe the Lord heard his cry and spared his life. This is just another reward for George's care for poor people. The amazing thing about that entire event is that at the time George was being recorded by a man he probably never realized loved him.

George Jones was full of mercy. Mercy was his gift, and he showed plenty of it. For that reason, he was blessed.

"Blessed are the merciful for they shall obtain mercy." Matthew 5:7

It grieves me to hear people tell stories about George that I know for a fact didn't happen. One popular tale is that George would be seen riding his lawn mower down the street to buy a bottle at the liquor store.

One guy living in Florence, Alabama said, "I lived next door to him, and he got on his lawn mower and drove it to a dealership and bought a car."

I heard another man say, "I lived down the road from George when he lived in Texas, and he got mad at Jimmy and rode his lawn mower down the road to get a drink."

This is the classic one: "George lived in Florida, got in bad financial shape and lost his car, so he rode his lawn mower to town."

I've never known a time in George's life when he could not afford a vehicle. Usually, he owned several at the same time not counting all the cars he bought for other people. False statements about George are what inspired me to write this book.

I feel that helping others was a form of nourishment to his soul. I never heard George complain one single time or make remarks of regret about helping others. If he had all the money and valuables he has given to his family, friends, strangers, charities, and other organizations, he would have probably tripled his wealth. If he had half of what he has been cheated out of, he would have had twenty times his wealth.

George was not a person who was comfortable fighting for his rights. He always said, "If they can live with it, I can live without it." And in reality, that's what he did. Most of those thieves have already faced death and will face judgment. Then what? *"Vengeance is mine, sayeth the Lord."* Romans 12:19

I've heard George quote that Scripture many times. I could sense a feeling of hurt, disappointment, a look of being betrayed, but he had learned to cope with such things after years of experiencing the hurt and pain. He was aware of certain people and keenly noticed if a person's motives were to help him or to exploit him. He hated crooks and deceitful people, but he was reluctant to confront them with their schemes. His awareness sometimes would keep him from making quick decisions or falling into traps that he perceived were laid out to hurt him. If there seemed to be no way out of a situation he didn't want to be in, he would just not show up for the hanging. Pretty smart!

I'm no judge, but I have a pretty good sense of a person's character. George was one of the very few people I could count on, and I always trusted him. It was extremely rare for me to rely on anybody, but I knew George was a trustworthy person when it came to common sense issues of life. Just because he wouldn't show up for a concert once-in-a-while didn't mean he would ever hurt me or disappoint me personally, and he never did. He was as loyal to Peanutt and me as we were to him, and he never once made us feel like he didn't want us around him even when the big dudes came to town. He was the same way with other people he loved. It was a shame that such a good person had to get messed up with a gang of thugs and crooks that led him astray from the person who lived within his soul.

....

CHAPTER SIXTEEN

The Dark Days of a White Substance

The sky could never produce a darker cloud than the one
that hung over George Jones during the time he was addicted to
cocaine. His mind was racing like a raging tornado sweeping across
the land and destroying everything in its path. It was devastating
to see the destruction this little white powder was doing to this
man's life. He had sunk so far into the darkness that it was doubtful
he would ever see the light of day again. His mind was so twisted
that he had lost all sense of direction. He was being tossed to and
fro like a bird caught in a whirlwind of destruction. He was being
destroyed in every area of his life. His career was being demolished,
his home life was wrecking, his longtime friendships were breaking
apart, and his business deals were failing.

George had gotten to the point where he didn't trust anybody...not even himself. He was totally confused about everybody
and everything. He no longer knew the difference between a friend
and an enemy. He didn't realize that the people who had always
loved him and stood by him through the good and the bad times
were still the people who were true and loyal to him.

George couldn't realize that there were evil people coming into his life who were exploiting his weaknesses and feeding
him cocaine like throwing corn to a starving hog. These were
the ones who were killing him a little bit every day. Each snort
was bringing him another sniff toward death. The sad part is that
they didn't care if they killed him. All they wanted was George on

cocaine, so they could get every dollar they could from him. They called themselves managers and believe me they were exactly that. They managed to drain the man of all his earnings, his career, his friends, and even his home life. The devils had no mercy on him; they had him in a place where he couldn't run and there was no place to hide. These so-called managers didn't want him involved with anyone they thought might try to help him get off cocaine. They supplied his habit even when he didn't have the money to buy it. They would force him to perform at concerts when he was barely able to stand up much less complete a performance. They couldn't have cared less how badly George felt, or how much it would damage his career; they only wanted to be paid for the cocaine he was using.

The people who really cared for George were hated by the suppliers. We were like somebody that would go into a department store and run off his or her best customers. George was a good user. If he didn't have the money, he would buy it on their credit until the next concert, and they would be right there to collect.

George and Linda had been together for several years and had gotten along really well until George started snorting cocaine. George became an entirely different person not only because of the cocaine, but because the dealers were always running down everybody around him. Nobody was good enough for George anymore; especially, Peanutt and me.

One of George's managers came to Linda and offered her thousands of dollars to leave George. She frankly told him she wouldn't leave George for any amount of money; she wasn't with him for money, and she sure wouldn't leave him for money. He told her that they could handle George better if she was not in his life. The whole deal was that they knew Linda was my sister, and they wanted rid of Peanutt, Linda, and me. They knew I had a lot of influence on George, and they wanted him right where they had him, messed up and under their control. George had no place to run except right back to them. He became extremely paranoid. He had been told so many lies that he didn't know who to believe, and who not to believe.

Peanutt and I had a little store in Florence where George would drop by every day or two and buy gas or just kill time. One day he stopped by, and I had a couple of ladies in the store shopping. He had been to Nashville earlier that day, and he arrived all messed up on cocaine. He had stopped by his house before he came to the store and had dressed up like an old man. He had not combed his hair and was wearing an old wide-brim felt hat with the trim around the brim hanging down around the edge of the hat. He was wearing a long, black overcoat with an expensive pair of Nudie cowboy boots. One boot was a bright orange, and the other was a bright apple green. He was carrying an old worn-out suitcase. I asked him what he was doing and he replied,

"They want me to be a bum, so here I am. I'm a bum, and I look like one don't I?"

Of course, I had to agree with him. I knew better than to disagree with George when he was messed up and especially when he had gone to so much trouble to prove his point. I have to admit that I felt really sorry for him. George was no fool, and I knew it. He was aware of what the vultures were doing to him, but he had gotten himself in so deep that he didn't know how to get out. As he sat there in the store talking about taking the horns off a Billy goat, one of the ladies made a comment about his boots.

"George, I really like that pair of boots," she commented.

"You really like my boots?" George asked.

"Yeah, I think they look great," she replied.

"Well, I tell you what. You can have this pair of boots. I have another pair just like these at home."

The lady was all excited that George Jones was going to give her his boots. I spoke up.

"No George, you can't give your boots away. You might have another pair just like them at home, but the pair at home are mismatched just like the boots you have on. It would be like giving away two pairs of your Nudie boots, and I can't let you do that."

The lady was disappointed with my input, but I knew that he would have regretted it later. George kept right on trying to pull his boots off to give them to her, so I finally told the lady she couldn't take them even if he took them off. I explained to her that they were very expensive boots and I didn't want her to take them from him and especially in my store. I assured her it was none of my business what he did elsewhere, but I couldn't let it happen there. She said she understood and finally left the store.

George stayed for a little while and then asked me to close the store and come over to his house; he had something he wanted to show me. I told him I'd close and would come on over in a little while. George was still messed up when he left.

I didn't close the store right then because I thought I had better wait on Peanutt to get there and go with me. I was a little afraid that George might be slightly unstable being in the frame of mind he was. He had been making remarks that were sarcastic, and it was hard to tell if they were meant for me or someone else.

The phone rang, and I answered it.

"Are you gonna close and come over here or not?" George asked.

"Yes, in a few minutes," I replied.

"I want you to come right now, this can't wait," George demanded.

I assured him I'd come on but instead I called Billy Robertson, a friend of Peanutt's and mine and asked him to go over to George's and see what was going on? I told Billy that George wanted me to come over, but I was afraid to go by myself with him all messed up.

Billy arrived at George's house, and George invited him in. They talked for a while and then Billy left. Billy called me at the store and advised me not to go. He said that George was in bad shape, and he didn't think it was a good idea for me to go over there alone. He said that George had a white sheet spread over his couch and a pillow at the end of the couch with an 8" x 10" picture of himself lying on the pillow. I continued trying to get in touch with Peanutt so we could go over there, but it had already gotten dark, and Peanutt was with a friend buying some recording equipment.

I was feeling a little guilty for not doing what I told George I would do, but I didn't fully trust George and his motives like I did before he got on cocaine. There had been many times I had gone to his house alone before he got so messed up, but then I knew I could trust him. I trusted George as much as I trusted my own brother, but I was not familiar with people on cocaine. I had never been around it until George got addicted, and he was not the man I had always known. We never did know what the sheet and pillow were about.

Linda had left earlier that day. George had called her from Nashville, and she could tell he was coked to the gill, and she didn't want to be there when he got home. She had become a little leery of him when he was messed up on that stuff. Sometimes, he would talk about people and make remarks, and you'd wonder if he was aiming it at you. With all the talk that was going on around him, you never knew what he had been told or how much of it he would believe under his circumstances. There were times when I was actually afraid of him. I knew George and knew him well, and there was nobody I would trust more than George. But, I had gotten to the point where I was afraid of the man cocaine had made of him. I witnessed him doing things and saying things that I knew beyond a shadow of doubt he wouldn't have done if he hadn't been on co-caine. That stuff would make Satan himself come out of a person, and I didn't trust the effects it can have on people.

George had started talking to himself about his friend, Don-ald Duck. He and Donald would carry on conversations with each other. George would ask Donald a question then he'd answer the question in a Donald Duck voice. He had practiced this so much that he could sound just like Donald Duck. They were buddies, and they made big plans to do certain things together. They'd scheme up things to do to the people they were mad at. They'd console each other as if they were a team working together.

The managers and cocaine dealers knew this was going on. They simply didn't care. George was like a gearshift to them. If they wanted him up, they'd shoot him up, literally. If they wanted him down, they put him down. They knew how to do that. If he wasn't moving fast enough, they'd throw him in overdrive. They nearly drove him to death. He was never left in neutral to idle. They couldn't allow him to slow down because they were afraid he might come to a stop, and they'd lose control. There were many stop signs for George, but he couldn't see them. He was blinded by the oncoming traffic.

The cocaine dealers knew George had friends who loved him and would encourage him to get off the substance. They knew he had family who loved him and were totally against his cocaine addiction. There were people in the music business that were against him using cocaine and warned him that it was ruining his career.

George finally gave his friend, "Donald Duck" some competition, he had created, "The Old Man." The old man was George's new friend. He went everywhere George went. He'd ride around with George and give George advice. He'd tell George stories about his life, and the two of them would make plans to do things together. George once told me about the old man.

"The old man nearly scared me to death. I had been driving down Highway 43 between Lawrenceburg and Florence. The old man showed up on top of my car. He had one leg hanging down through the sunroof, and the other leg was laid across the front fender of my car. I knew I had left him in Nashville, and I can't understand how he got on top of my car, but all of a sudden, he was right there with me!"

"Maybe," I explained, "He's an angel and has wings and can fly as fast as you can drive? Maybe he was flying over your car all the time and decided to land on your car."

"That's the only way it could have happened," George said, "An angel? If that old man is an angel, he's the only Godly thing around me."

It was a real confused time for George. It was a lonely time as well. I really felt sorry for him, but it was beyond anything we could do to help him. Before George had gotten on cocaine, he had gone to church with Peanutt and me a few times at First Freewill Baptist on Florence Boulevard. Brother Tom Malone was the pastor there. George really liked Bro. Tom. One evening, George wanted us to ride our motorcycles and wanted Bro. Tom to ride with us. Bro. Tom brought along his daughter, Maryanne, and we went riding. Bro. Tom talked to George about his relationship with the Lord, but not in such a way that it would be offensive to George. George listened because Bro. Tom was not preachy and very effective. We went back to Bro. Tom's church several times. George said he enjoyed the services but never made any kind of commitment.

Peanutt started pastoring his own church, The Lord's Chapel in Sheffield, Alabama. George visited our church a couple of times. One night, George called up and said he wanted us to come to his house. When we arrived there, George wanted Peanutt to pray with him, and George gave Peanutt a check for $5000.00 he said was for the church.

"Peanutt, I want to give this to your church," George said when he gave it to him. We didn't really understand why, but we accepted it. Some folks have made fun of Peanutt and made slurry remarks about Peanutt sermonizing George. They've even made fun of his calling to preach, but it never bothered Peanutt. He knows where he stands, and he'll continue to stand on the Solid Rock.

George came to the place where he would ask Peanutt questions about God and the Bible. Peanutt was a new Christian himself, and sometimes he wouldn't know exactly how to answer a loaded question. George decided to go with Peanutt to a tent revival held by Bro. Tony Staggs from Russellville, Alabama. There was a big tent set up on top of Hawk Pride Mountain, just out of

Tuscumbia city limits. It was drizzling rain that night. Peanutt and George got out of the car and knelt down beside it. The rain began to fall even heavier. George and Peanutt knelt there listening to the preacher. No one had any idea that George Jones was outside that tent listening to the preaching and singing. George asked Peanutt to move up a little closer to the tent because he wanted to feel like he was a part of the service. They moved in closer. Tears began rolling down George's face. Peanutt's heart started pounding. He knew George had felt a stirring in his soul. Peanutt was sitting on pins and needles. He was in high hopes that George might surrender to the Lord. Just about the time Peanutt thought George was ready to make a move toward the altar inside the tent, a man came out and recognized George and blurted out to everybody that George Jones was outside. George was then ready to go, and so was Peanutt. Peanutt had to get George out of there. He knew there would be more damage done than good. They left the mountain service before the service was over to keep George from being confronted by a lot of people.

After George's near miss at becoming a Christian at the tent revival that night, the Devil really went to work on him. The Devil knew he nearly lost George, so he started planting all sorts of stuff in George's head. He truly was scrambling up George's mind. George began to resent Peanutt being a Christian. He would call Peanutt and tell him he was coming over to our house to discuss the Bible. George would show up and rattle off unanswerable questions. He wanted to debate the Bible, and many times he would leave our house furious.

One time, he brought a beautiful bright red Bible with him. It had been autographed to George from Bob Herrington, whose title was "The Chaplain of Bourbon Street" at that time and who was a popular evangelist. George brought the Bible in and turned to some scriptures that he had been reading and asked Peanutt what he thought about that particular scripture? Peanutt explained to the best of his ability what the scripture meant. Of course, George disagreed with every explanation Peanutt gave to him. "Where is God? Why don't he come down here right now and let me see him? Why does he hide from me? Is he a dictator? I don't understand why he don't come to me and show himself to me like he did to you?" George said angrily.

The more Peanutt tried to explain what the Scriptures meant, the more furious George would become. Finally, George grabbed the red Bible and started ripping pages out of it. He opened the door and threw it into the yard. He stormed from the house in a rage. We picked the pretty Bible up and kept it, and we still have it to this day.

George went to Nashville for a few days and then came home. He was in a good mood, but that only lasted about three days. He said he was going to the barbershop and when he came home, he was all messed up again. George had different moods that would show up depending on what he was ingesting into his system. He came home in his traveling mood and asked Linda to drive him to Florida. It was already pretty late in the day. Linda reluctantly agreed to drive him to Lakeland, Florida although she was dreading it. It only took thirty minutes to pack and get in the car, and Linda barely had time to get her necessities together. When they arrived in Montgomery, Alabama, George changed his mind and wanted to go home. Linda had been driving for five hours and was tired. It was already after midnight, and she would have to turn around and drive five more hours.

They made it to Birmingham, and Linda insisted that George find a room. She said she couldn't drive any longer and was afraid she'd fall asleep at the wheel. George told her to pull into the next motel she came to, and they'd get a room. When they woke up the next morning, they showered and went to the car. By the time Linda had started the car, George had decided he wanted to go on to Florida. He told Linda to head towards Lakeland.

George had been snorting a little cocaine off and on all day. He was beginning to get really messed up, and Linda was getting really worried. He told her to pull into a service station and fill up with gas. Linda did as she was told and when the attendant had finished filling the car, he went inside to pay for the gas. For some reason, George walked into the station garage and started giving out $100 bills to the boys working there. The boys were in shock, and they didn't seem to know who George was.

It wasn't long after they were on the road heading south toward Florida that Linda became very tired from her lack of sleep. At the same time, George was getting more and more messed up. About fifty miles down the road from where they had bought gas, George said he wanted Linda to pull off the Interstate and park on the side of the road. Linda told him she wouldn't do it because she would get a ticket for stopping on the Interstate. She had no idea why he wanted her to stop, but she relented and pulled off to the side of the road.

George blatantly asked her to snort cocaine. Linda told him in no uncertain terms that she would never use cocaine. He was aggravated at her and told her it wouldn't hurt her if she tried it. Linda flatly refused and started making excuses that she was sleepy and had to make good time on the road while she could stay awake. Even though George was upset at her, he didn't push the issue and gave up asking.

They reached the Florida state line, and Linda realized she had to get off the road and get some sleep. She also knew that George was getting higher and higher on the substance, and she didn't know what to expect from him.

"George," Linda said, "I've got to get some sleep, I'm exhausted. I've got to lay down." George agreed to stop at the next motel they found, and they both slept until the next morning.

George woke up at 6:00 a.m. and then showered. He woke Linda as soon as he was finished and told her to hurry up and get her shower and get dressed because he wanted to get to Lakeland as soon as he could. Linda dressed in shorts thinking it was going to be warm down in Lakeland. She drove away from the motel but only traveled about twenty-five miles when George said he wanted to stop and get something to eat.

They stopped at a Kentucky Fried Chicken and when they got back in the car, George said,

"Linda, let's go back home, I don't want to go to Lakeland. We'll come back down here next week."

Linda was not all that upset at this sudden behavioral change because she didn't know what she would be confronted with once she got to Lakeland. She knew she could call Cliff and Maxine Hider if she had to. They were good friends with George and Tammy. Linda had met them, and she really liked both of them and felt she could call them if she needed to.

On the other hand, Linda dreaded the long trip home. She was already worn out, so she made up her mind that she was driving all the way home no matter if George liked it or not. She was going home, and she was going to stay when she got there. She drove back to Florence without stopping except for gas and something to eat, and every mile of the way she was thinking, *"He'll never get to do this to me again. If he goes to Florida, someone else will have to take him. It won't be me."* They made it home.

Linda called and wanted Peanutt and me to go check on George. She said she had left him home alone. He was messed up, so she went to my mother's house rather than staying with him in that condition. We found George at home, and he had been snorting cocaine.

Peanutt convinced George to go to Danvers Restaurant with us to eat some chicken. Peanutt picked Danvers because at that time of night there wouldn't be many people there. The few people who were there recognized George but didn't bother him. It was easy for anybody to see he was not in very good shape.

Our food was on the table and just as we began to eat, all of a sudden George shoved his face down into his plate and picked up a piece of chicken with his teeth. He started shaking it from side-to-side like a wild animal would. Peanutt convinced him to stop making a fool of himself. I think George was doing it because he felt like someone might have been watching him, and it ticked him off. It didn't take much to put him in the foulest of moods when he was coked up. We left the restaurant and took George home with us because we knew Linda was not coming home.

Peanutt realized that something was going to have to be done with George. He was getting worse all the time and was running like a wild animal from place to place and never happy anywhere he went. One night about 7:00 p.m., the phone rang. It was George. He was crying.

"Peanutt, come over here. You've got to pray with me." George cried.

We immediately went to George's house. He was still weeping when we got there.

"Peanutt, I was in Nashville and a light came into my room. It scared me, but I know it was a light from God. You've got to pray with me, and help me become a Christian." The three of us joined hands, and Peanutt began to pray for George. Peanutt and I knew George probably better than anyone else, and we knew this time he was as sincere as he'd ever been in his life. The next day, we tried to call Jimmy Swaggart because George had been watching Jimmy Swaggart on TV when the light came into his room. We never talked to Mr. Swaggart because his "gate keepers" just kept passing us from secretary to secretary. Finally, we wound up with a girl who happened to be from Florence, Alabama, and she knew us. We explained our situation to her and told her that we needed Mr. Swaggart to talk to George. We were surprised that Jimmy Swaggart would not make himself available; especially, since this was George Jones calling and not some person who wanted to waste his time. We asked her to please have him return our call but to this day, he has never called us. We were very let down and disappointed because we felt that maybe he could have helped lead George to Christ.

After the prayer, George testified that he felt better about himself. He was straight for several weeks and was doing much better. The vultures couldn't stand it. They came sneaking back into his life, and it wasn't long until George was patronizing the bowling alley on Florence Boulevard a bit too often.

George wanted us to go bowling with him, so we would go and begin playing a game. George would start the game and then make excuses as to why he needed to step away for a while. We watched him going into a room at the back of the alley. When he emerged from his secret place, he would be so messed up that he'd make us quit in the middle of the game and take him home.

We had been going to the bowling alley and bowling with George since the day he moved to Florence. We loved to bowl and always had a good time because George was straight and a lot of fun.

When the bowling alley was brought under new ownership, something went wrong, and everything changed almost overnight. It took us a while to realize that the purpose of going to the bowling alley was not to bowl. By the time we figured it out, it was too late.

George was our life, and it had always been fun to go bowling, hang out at the Moose Lodge, play bingo, camp out, fish, play volleyball, play Aggravation, go on trips, hunt, or just sit around the house and watch TV.

Cocaine and its suppliers had robbed George of all the fun things we did together as a family. It had all been destroyed. George was really happy in those days, but they had to mess him up. It was the master plan of the ones who were hungry for money that got him addicted to cocaine, and then stole every dollar they could from him. The more he gave to them, the more they wanted. They didn't want George to get his head on straight and didn't care if his act was together. They didn't want him to have a decent life. They wanted control of him, his career, his money, and anything else they could get from him. The hell with his life, his health, his friends, his family, and even his soul.

George was a dying man. He only weighed a scrawny 98 pounds, and we knew something had to be done for him. He became more and more dependent on cocaine and became totally paranoid. We desperately wanted to help him, but we were unsure of the route we needed to take.

George had gotten more and more dependent on cocaine, while he was becoming more and more paranoid. He had completely lost self-control, dignity, and any confidence in himself. He had become extremely jealous of anyone who was a friend to us because he thought we were putting someone else above him. I guess it seemed that way because we had been spending more time with other friends and not a lot of time with him.

Peanutt and I were getting so many threats coming in by phone warning us to stay away from George that we had to pay attention and cut back the time we were spending with him. Those calls were real and threatening. We never totally shared with George how badly we were afraid for our own lives and his. It was way worse than George realized.

One evening, I had planned to go to a Home Interiors party at my best friend's house that was scheduled to begin at 7:00 p.m. Peanutt had business to take care of, so I went on to the party. George knew that I spent a lot of time with Barbara Robertson, and he knew that I was going to be at her house that night. George had been to Nashville and when he returned home, he called my house. Of course I wasn't there, so he called me at Barbara's, and the phone rang halfway through the party. George asked Barbara to get me on the phone.

"Where is little Jesus?" George asked when I answered.

"Who are you talking about?" I asked him.

"You know little Jesus, Peanutt-you know little Jesus," he slurred.

I could tell George was stoned, and I could tell he was angry. I told him that Peanutt was gone to take care of some business and would be home later on. He called me four or five times that night wanting to know if I had heard from little Jesus. Each time I talked to him, I could feel more and more anger in his voice.

"I want to find that little Jesus and pluck his beard hairs out one by one." George yelled.

I had never heard George talk like this before. It scared me because he sounded so different and strange. I had never heard George talk about anyone the way he was talking about Peanutt. I kept calling home, so I could warn Peanutt of George's condition.

"Peanutt, don't answer if George calls." I said when Peanutt finally answered the phone. "He's in bad shape and is mad at us about something. He is calling you little Jesus and said he wanted to hold you down and pluck your beard hairs out one by one so please stay away from him tonight. He's threatening you."

Peanutt and I were getting an excessive number of threatening phone calls, so we were staying away from home as much as possible. We were trying to avoid danger to our daughter and us. That night, we decided to stay at home, and George kept calling until Peanutt finally answered the phone.

"Peanutt, I want you to come over to my house." George demanded.

Peanutt told him "no" that he wasn't going to his house.

"Then meet me below Shoals Creek Bridge down by the creekside." George instructed Peanutt.

For some reason, Peanutt agreed to meet George at the bridge. He arrived before George did. Peanutt drove across the bridge and while waiting on George to show up, he asked God to protect him from any kind of harm. George came over the bridge and then pulled his car down by the creek. Peanutt rolled down his window, turned his body so that he was facing George, and laid both arms on the top of the door.

George rolled down his window and wildly stared at Peanutt.

"See if your God can save you now!" George yelled as he pointed the .38 caliber pistol squarely at Peanutt's head.

George pulled the trigger, but he missed his shot, and the bullet ricocheted off a metal piece exposed when the window was rolled down, and then lodged in the door between Peanutt's hands and his face. If the bullet had not lodged in the top of the door just below the window, it would have hit Peanutt in the heart and most likely would have killed him. God spared his life.

"I ought to kill you right here, you letting your wife have an affair right under your nose, and you ain't doing anything about it" George coldly said as he cocked the pistol's hammer and got ready to pull the trigger again.

Peanutt had a pistol in the seat of his car and was going to fire at George but decided he would not hurt him. George began to sling his gun around and was shouting all kinds of threatening things to Peanutt.

"I'm going to the house." George said as he put his pistol on the seat beside him and drove away.

Peanutt went straight to the police department and filed a complaint. They swore out a warrant for attempted murder against George. George was arrested three days later. He was released after posting a $2,500.00 bond. We had no intention of sending George to prison, but we wanted him to think he might have to go. We wanted to shake him up to wake him up, so he would become aware of the shape he had gotten himself into. We let the case ride until it was time to show up in Court.

Peanutt went to court with George and stood up before Judge Druska. He told the judge that he didn't want George to go to prison, and that he wanted to drop the charges against George and not prosecute him. (The DA had told us George could get 15 years in prison) Peanutt had a restraining order filed on George that ordered him to stay away from us when he was under the influence of drugs and alcohol.

George weighed less than 100 pounds when he walked into the courtroom. He looked pitiful.

"I'm guilty, what else can I say? I'm sorry, I'm guilty." George told the judge.

The judge told him that Peanutt had chosen to drop all charges against him, but that he would not be allowed to come back around us while under the influence of alcohol or drugs nor while carrying a weapon. George agreed to abide by the restraining order, and then court was dismissed.

We didn't see George for a couple of weeks. Then one day, he showed up and knocked on the door.

"Well, I threw my pistol away and got rid of all my other guns, and I never intend to own another one, and I've quit drinking and messing around with cocaine. I've been missing you, and I wanted to come and see you. I hope it's okay."

We asked George to come in and assured him it was okay for him to be there. We were happy to see him. We thought he had been drinking and was pretty high right then, but we knew he'd be fine. He came in and asked me to put on the old 45 record of Maybelline, so I put it on the record player. It was playing pretty loud, and George jumped up and started dancing around to the music, and his pistol fell out of his boot. He had that "I got caught with my hand in the cookie jar grin" realizing he had been caught in a lie.

"Oh, yeah," I said, "You threw it away all right, just like you've quit drinking. You're half drunk right now."

He laughed and made a joke out of it and asked me if I was going to call the law on him? I told him no, it was okay for him to be there and okay for him to have the pistol on him.

"I just don't want any alcohol or drugs in the house, okay?" I said.

"Okay." He replied. He stayed all day with us and when it started to get dark, he asked if he could spend the night. We told him it would be fine, and that we would love for him to stay.

I think he was just testing us to see if we would let him stay or to see if we still trusted him. He found out that we did trust him, and that we still loved him and wanted to be with him but not when he was under the influence of cocaine.

George got up the next morning before we did, and when we got up, he was gone. I went into his room to make up the bed. Sitting beside the bed was a half-empty pint of Jack Daniels whiskey. George just had to break the rules we had set for him. He wanted to let us know that he wasn't going to abide by any court orders. I knew George well enough to believe he really didn't mean any harm. He had too much pride to let us put a condition on our relationship. From then on, George came and went as he pleased, and we never had any more trouble with him.

From time to time, people would ask me if I was mad at George for accusing me of having an affair. I simply told them that I had probably said or done things that made George think he was telling the truth, or someone else had led him to believe that it was the truth.

I had spent a lot of time with a friend because he couldn't read, and I'd read his mail for him and finally went into business with him. I suppose it did look suspicious to some folks. He was a person I knew I could trust, and someone I knew I could depend on in a time of need. Both of us were married; his wife was also my friend, and Peanutt was a friend with both of them. We all did a lot of things together that included George and Linda. We took trips to Florida and several other places. There were times I could tell that George didn't want them traveling with us. He was happier when it was only Peanutt, Linda, and me with him. I always wanted another couple with us in case George decided to goof off.

George became a little jealous of the other couple. He probably wasn't the only one who had bad thoughts about me and the other person, but frankly, I didn't care what people thought. I didn't care what it looked like. Peanutt knew our friend well enough to know that nothing was going on between us. In fact, the man was one of the first to witness to Peanutt about Jesus.

We stopped by his business one day and made a purchase, and he gave Peanutt a Bible. It made Peanutt stop and think. This was before Peanutt became a Christian. This man always talked to Peanutt about his drinking; he'd encourage him not to drink. This man's wife was an alcoholic, and he knew how it was to have to tolerate a drunk, so I appreciated him trying to talk to Peanutt about his drinking. Most everybody would encourage Peanutt to drink, so I needed this person to be around Peanutt. I really pushed the issue of being friends with him. Did it work?

Regardless of all the gossip, in spite of all the false accusations concerning an affair, the end result was that Peanutt became a Christian and completely gave up drinking and had nothing to do with alcohol from that day forward. Booze no longer controlled Peanutt's life.

We did allow George to visit us when he was drinking, but he was the only person who had that privilege. We loved George, and we knew if we were to have any kind of relationship with him, we would have to tolerate his habits. Am I angry with George for accusing me of an affair? No, I'm not mad and have not been mad at George over what he said to Peanutt. I probably caused it myself. In any case, I still love George, and I realized the shape he was in at the time. He was all messed up and confused. Evil people influenced him into believing anything and everything they wanted him to believe. I have forgiven him a long time ago for trying to kill my husband. I placed it all in God's hands.

I hold no grudges against anyone. George was the person who taught me that it is wrong to hold a grudge. When Peanutt and I got married, I was really young, still in my teens, and George was talking about someone he had been mad at.

"Oh, I'm not mad at him now," George explained. "You know, it's wrong to hold a grudge against someone."

That really impressed me. I remember thinking, *"That's a soft-hearted man."* It made me respect him; even though, I hardly knew him at the time, but I'll never forget it, or where he said it. We were at the Biltmore Hotel in Nashville waiting on studio time, so George could record some songs.

Time went on, and George continued to use cocaine and alcohol. He'd make frequent trips back and forth from Florence to Nashville. We never knew what kind of shape he'd be in when he arrived home, but we never expected it to be good, and it never was. George became more and more unpredictable, and everyone around him was afraid of him. He was mad at everybody, including his managers and cocaine suppliers. He was angry at the world. He didn't believe or have confidence in anybody. He did weird things like make a list of people that he was going to kill. George first showed me this list, and I was somewhat shocked at the violence that seemed to be inside of him, and yet I knew him. I knew there was no intent to harm these people, but we had to take him serious because he did attempt to kill Peanutt. There were six names on the list; Tammy Wynette, George Richey, Paul Richey, Shug Baggot, Billy Sherrill, and Shorty Lavender. Even though we had to pay attention to George's paranoia, we knew that cocaine was the driving force behind his anger.

George came by our store one afternoon driving a 1979 white Thunderbird Landau. He pulled up in front of the store and honked his horn. I went out to see him.

"Well, the next time you'll see me, I'll be in a coffin," he said to me.

"What do you mean, George?" I asked quietly.

"Just what I said," he replied. He shoved the gearshift in drive and sped out of the parking lot slinging gravel everywhere.

I told Peanutt what George had said and done.

"I've got to get George some help," Peanutt said. "I don't know what I'm gonna do, but I've got to do something before someone gets hurt, or he hurts himself. I've made up my mind, and I'm not gonna back up. It don't look like anybody cares if he lives or dies, and I'm gonna get help for him; it's for his own good."

Peanutt was really upset. He was afraid George might try to kill himself, or maybe someone had threatened George, and he was trying to clue us in on it.

Peanutt left the store and while he was on the way out, he told me he was going to see what he could do to get George some help.

"Even you know he's gonna get hurt if I don't do something, and I'm not gonna sit back and let it happen." Peanutt explained.

Peanutt went to visit Judge Duncan. He told the Judge about George's condition. He explained to him that he'd been as close to George as his own family for years, and that George's family lived in Texas, but they were too far away to help him. He assured the Judge that George's family members would help him if they could, but George wouldn't listen to them or cooperate no matter how hard they would try to help him. It would be too difficult for them to make frequent trips to Alabama. Peanutt told the Judge that he wanted to be George's Power of Attorney, so he could have him committed. The Judge agreed on the grounds that George had become too incompetent to handle his own affairs. Peanutt signed the documents and also signed papers to have George arrested and committed to the rehab center in Florence. The Sheriff was sent to arrest George and take him to the Riverbend Hospital in Florence, Alabama. Riverbend kept him for three days, and then transferred George to the Hillcrest Hospital in Birmingham, Alabama. Dr. Knuckles was his Doctor at Hillcrest, and he gave the hospital staff strict orders that no one was to see George except Peanutt, Linda, and me.

Peanutt called Tammy Wynette and told her that he had had George committed, and where he was at the time. Peanutt had to put up $1,000.00 to get him admitted, but it was going to cost $10,000.00 for him to stay 30 days. Tammy said she'd get the money together for the rest of the bill. George was there about six days before we went to see him. When we walked into his little room, he was sitting in the corner all puffed up at us.

"Why did you do this to me?" He asked Peanutt.

"George," Peanutt replied, "I did it because I love you. You were going to die if somebody didn't help you."

George was still aggravated when we left. On the third day George was in the hospital, he called.

"Peanutt, bring me a few dollars down here and a belt and some cigarettes." George demanded.

Peanutt told him that we'd bring the stuff that day. We took the money and cigarettes to George, but they wouldn't allow him to have the belt. George was in a much better mood when we visited him. He was rooming with an older man, who read the Bible all the time. George was fond of the little old man.

We visited George often because he was allowed no other visitors. The doctors were afraid that someone might sneak cocaine to him. Near the end of George's stay at Hillcrest, he talked to us a lot about what he was going to do when he got out of the hospital.

"I have no place to go; I don't have a home to go to," he would opine.

He had been renting an apartment at the time he was committed because Linda had given up their apartment and moved in with Peanutt and me.

"Linda has left me, and I don't have a home, and I ain't got no furniture." George cried.

Linda took his hand and assured him that if he'd stay off cocaine, she'd come back to him. She told him that she'd only left him because of the cocaine addiction and couldn't tolerate the situation any longer. We told him that we had a friend who built really nice houses, and we'd convince him to sell George a house with nothing down until he could get on his feet again. George didn't think anyone would sell him a house without a down payment.

"Oh yeah, he will, trust me," I said. "I can call him tomorrow and find out what he has for sale." I knew Ronald Warren had just built some really nice homes in the Creekwood Subdivision.

"What do I do about furnishing it?" George asked.

I told him that I had a friend who owned a big furniture store, and that I would cosign to get all the furniture he needed for his house on a credit account. George refused to believe it could be done, but he told us to let him know if we could work it out.

On the way home, we talked with Linda about all the plans. We assured her that George really wanted her to come back and asked her to please give him another chance. She said the only way she would consider it is if George stayed away from cocaine.

I called Ronald Warren (the builder) and told him of George's condition and situation. I told him I wanted to see some houses, and that we wanted to buy one for George and explained to him that George had been in the hospital and couldn't make a down payment. I told the builder that George was good for the money and would make a down payment as soon as he got back to work, and that we'd get a loan for the rest. Mr. Warren showed Linda and I a nice house, so we bought it on the spot. I called United Furniture Store in Sheffield and asked to speak to Dewey Parker. He was another good friend of mine. I told Dewey the same thing I told Ronald about George's situation. I asked him to let me cosign a loan to buy George some furniture on credit and if he would, that we'd buy everything George needed for his house from United Furniture.

Dewey Parker was delighted to let Linda and me shop and buy whatever we wanted. I told him that if George didn't like certain things we picked out, that we expected him to let George trade it for something else. He agreed to that. Linda and I spent almost the whole day in the furniture store trying to decide what George would like for the house.

We finished shopping after a long day and asked that the items be delivered in three days. The carpet and wallpaper were finished, the furniture had been delivered, Linda had moved in, and George came home. He liked the house, he liked most of the furniture, and he was very happy that Linda had come back to him. He was happy to be home. He clearly understood why Peanutt had him committed to the hospital. The Doctor explained to George that he would not have lived more than thirty days if he had not gotten some help. George very much appreciated what Peanutt had done for him.

George stayed straight. He changed managers and went back to work on the road. He finally made the down payment on the house, paid off the furniture, and was doing really well. He had gained a little weight and looked better than he had in a long time. Linda was happy with George. She knew he had straightened up and was trying hard to get a new start. George applied for a loan on his house that got approved and closed.

For several months all was going well, but one day out of the clear blue, George and his new manager had a few words. The vultures, that knew George's weaknesses, showed up. They knew if they could catch him at the right time, he'd be conquerable. A short time after they had sunk their talons into his flesh, George was back snorting dope. It was heartbreaking to see him fall back into this old trap and routine.

George wasn't using the substance quite as badly as he had been before. He'd do coke, but not all the time. He'd stay straight for days before he's get messed up again.

George again resigned his former manager, and Wayne Oliver became his new manager. Wayne was good for George. This relationship led to George becoming involved with Gerald Murray of Muscle Shoals. Gerald became George's manager for a while, and Wayne Oliver became his road manager.

Peanutt and I moved from Florence to Muscle Shoals, so that George and Linda could sell their house and move there also. George liked being close to us, and we liked being close to him.

There are many, many things I loved about George that gave him that simple humble charm that most big stars don't possess. Most of them believe the world owes them a living, and that they deserve all the fanfare, money, and fortune. George was not that person.

George always stressed that he was just a simple country-man, who wanted to live a simple life. The entire glamor in the world could never take the country out of him. A gourmet meal to George was a pot of white Beaus with an onion, a chopped bell pepper thrown in, and pone of cornbread. Fancy meals didn't suit him. He was totally happy with a pot of dumplings or a bowl of potato soup. Top that off with chocolate pie or banana pudding, and he was happy.

When we'd go out to eat, it was not surprising that George

would always choose places that served country food. He was fond of Morrison's Café, and every few days we'd have to stop in and have some good old country cooking. Stan's Restaurant in Spring Hill, Tennessee was a regular eating place on our way to and from Nashville. You could get a bowl of pintos or white Beaus with a large piece of crackling cornbread and a slab of real country ham with redeye gravy.

In Florence where George lived for almost eight years, we'd hit steak houses that had a hot bar with all kinds of veggies, meats, salads, sweets, and ice cream. George never liked to dress up and go out to eat. He only wanted to be one of the crowd and was almost embarrassed about the status he had attained in the Country Music world. He'd sometimes wear blue jeans, a cotton shirt, and tennis shoes. George wanted to be comfortable, and he didn't care about how much someone was impressed by him. In the event that someone recognized him in a restaurant, he'd be nice but didn't let his food get cold trying to appease anyone. He was a down to earth man and resisted every effort to change.

....

CHAPTER SEVENTEEN

Nancy Sepulvado, Wife Number Five

While on a tour in Louisiana, Wayne Oliver, George's Manager, introduced him to Nancy Sepulvado. Nancy came into George's life at the time he was suffering from cocaine addiction, confusion, and paranoia, and this created a very turbulent relationship in the beginning. I don't think there could have been a worse time for someone to become involved with George. He was bent completely out of shape emotionally and physically. George was not the man we knew and loved; he became a stranger, and that affected his lifelong friendship with Peanutt and me.

Nancy also came into his life at a time when he desperately needed someone to love. He needed someone who could and would face all the consequences that were coming at him from every direction, and that's exactly what Nancy did.

Nancy got in touch with every so-called friend George had and put each one on notice to stay out of George's way, or there would be hell to pay. She took no chances, so she called every person acquainted with him. She was shooting bullets into the crowd, and there was no one who didn't feel the pellets. Whatever it took for her to hang onto George, that's what she did. She didn't care who was who, or who had been what? She didn't care how many people she had to hurt; she put them on their way out of George's life. She built a hedge around George, and she guarded him like a warden would guard a prisoner.

Nancy cleaned house. She stopped so-called friends and

strangers from popping up at the door any time they felt like it, and she took control of the managers. It took her a long time to convince George that she was really trying to help him because he was not accepting her wiping the slate clean very easily and gave her a hard time about taking so much control. Once George realized Nancy really loved him and wanted to help him get his life back in order, he decided to marry her. He realized he had a woman that would go to hell and back for him. She went through every kind of trial imaginable to prove that she was the real thing.

Nancy was brand new in George's life, so she didn't have a history of information to draw from. She inherited a mess that had to be straightened out. She didn't know exactly whom she could trust, and it didn't take her long to figure out some of the moves she needed to make, and she made them. I was surprised that she chose to be friends with a couple of people who had been very close to Peanutt and me. The most surprising was the friendship she had with my sister, Linda, who was George's fourth wife.

George and Nancy moved to Texas, and that's when he asked Nancy to marry him. Helen is George's sister, and they were married at her house. Helen was very fond of Nancy, and she was happy that George had found happiness with her. She had worried about George so much when he was so badly addicted to cocaine, and she felt that Nancy was going to be the key to the happiness she so much wanted for him.

George's Texas Park was going good, and all avenues of George's life seemed to be straightening out.

George left the East Texas area and moved to Nashville. Nancy stuck by his side every inch of the way. They moved to a farm in Franklin, Tennessee and were living there when George passed away. He was married to Nancy longer than he was any of his other wives. George did nothing but prosper after he met and married Nancy. His whole life changed. He enjoyed being at home, watching ball games, performing on stage, and he loved being around the horses on the farm with Nancy and his grandkids.

He developed a great relationship with his daughter, Georgette. They recorded a great song as a duet *"You and Me and Time."* I love it. They did an excellent job singing together, and it brought tears to my eyes and chill bumps to my arms when I first heard it. George was sober, off cocaine, free of managers, and finally found the peace he had been seeking for a very long time. He was at last a happy man.

I didn't know very much about Nancy. She never wanted to be associated with us, and we were among the list of George's friends she cut loose with the ties. I really don't blame her because she didn't know us, and she was taking no chances with anyone who had previously been associated with George.

I was hurt by her decision at first, and I didn't know if she was real or just another gold digger looking for what she could get from George. After seeing what she was willing to go through to get George back on his feet, I then began to appreciate her and realized that she really loved George Jones.

Nancy has proven to be the best thing that ever happened to George. I know she hurt the feelings of a lot people but when you have your hands full with the challenge of straightening out a legend like George Jones, you don't need a lot of extra weight on your shoulders. Nancy did what she felt was best for George Jones, and that's the kind of person he needed in his life. I firmly believe that Nancy saw through the mess George was in and saw the good side of him. I believe she knew he was a good man that needed help. She was so right.

George got lucky because whatever she did worked. George knew that Nancy had been a lifesaver for him. He needed her as much as a baby needs a mama. She handled his business and got him back into the financial status he deserved. They will always have our love and our blessings.

··

CHAPTER EIGHTEEN

What My Woman Can't Do,
Can't Be Done

Nancy strikes me as a person that flat doesn't care what other people may think of her when she's on a mission; especially when it came to taking care of George. That's exactly the way I have always been by Peanutt. It worked for me, and it's worked for Nancy. My theory has always been, "Don't put something you love on the table if you don't want someone else to take it." Tammy sang a song that says *"Good Loving Keeps a Home Together,"* but it takes a whole lot more than good loving for a home to survive. It takes many things like being strong enough to bend as Tanya Tucker sings. It takes hard work, and it takes being committed and dedicated to the one you love. It takes being tough but having a forgiving spirit and laying a firm foundation and building on it.

Peanutt wrote the song, *"What My Woman Can't Do, Can't Be Done."* He said he wrote it about me. George is a co-writer of that song, and I believe he felt that same way about Nancy. I fought like a tiger in the beginning of our marriage to keep it together. Peanutt drank like George did, and it made it hard on me. He'd slip off in the middle of the night while I was asleep to go get something to drink. I had to wait until I knew he was sound asleep before I'd take my bath in fear he would leave while I was in the tub. I couldn't even go shopping and leave him at home. I knew he wouldn't be there when I got back. I quit going anywhere without Peanutt. I wouldn't let him go to the store to get a pack of cigarettes unless I was with him. Sometimes he'd tell me I couldn't go, but I'd go anyway. We'd get mad at each other, but I didn't care. I made a lot of his buddies mad at me, but I couldn't care less. It has all paid off in the long run.

George upheld Nancy for all she did for him. Peanutt now tells everybody that if it hadn't been for me, he would be dead. It's the truth. George and Peanutt were living hard and would have died young if their lives had not turned around. I have no regrets for the way I have been with Peanutt. People have said that I was overly jealous of Peanutt, but that's not true. I was only jealous when I had a right to be. I'd tell someone off in a heart beat and put them in line, or I'd put them on their way. I just didn't tolerate a bunch of horse manure. I admire Nancy for the strong hold she took on George's life and his career; she saved them both, however, what I am appalled about is the way she treated his children during her marriage with George and after his death.

··

CHAPTER NINETEEN

A Day of Reckoning

The storm had passed; the damage had been done. Things were not the same. Friendships had been destroyed, homes had been demolished, and hearts had been broken. People had been hurt, and some had been killed. All through the years that I knew George Jones, I'd hear him discuss different people that had cheated him out of royalties, beat him out of credits, took him on deals, swindled him out of money, conned him out of valuable things, and took advantage of him when he was stoned on drugs, and he'd always say,

"Well, there's one thing about it. There's a day of reckoning."

The Bible speaks of a day of reckoning. It reads about a time when people will have to answer for the things they've done wrong towards their fellow man. For every cent of George's royalties that he's been cheated of, someone will have to face Jesus Christ and give an account for every valuable thing that has been taken wrongfully. Those insidious thieves who got George Jones hooked on cocaine and then stole his goods will face the Judge of Judges and give an account for what they've done. They will face judgment and get what they deserve.

George was not only damaged but the entire world that revolved around him. It hurt everybody. The damage drugs had on George will never be forgotten or repaired. It's not fair to those that really loved George and cared for him. I know we all have to forgive people, but sometimes I find it rather hard to forgive someone who deliberately hurts others.

The Lord will recognize each person for what he or she really is. He will reveal each person's motives, He will reveal how people conspired to get their way, and He will reveal the truth behind every lie. George Jones was mistreated by many people throughout his life and career. He might be George Jones the Country Music Legend, but he felt emotional pain just like all the rest of us. His feelings were just as sensitive as anybody else's feelings, but he is a legend, and every reaction was a story for the National news, a sleazy tabloid, and every other source of gossip that exists on the planet. George was hurt deeply by all the lies that could never be undone, and the truth setting the record straight.

Put yourself in George's shoes for a day and you will learn a lot about what it is to be a legend. It's not easy. It's a blessing, but it's also a job. Imagine how it would be if you went out to dine at a fine restaurant with your wife and some friends, your favorite food had just been served, you're ready to eat and enjoy yourself, you look up, and all you can see is an army of people coming to your table waving their pens and papers and asking you for an autograph. They will stand around talking for ten minutes about the last concert they attended, and how great it was. The food gets cold, the evening is not spent the way it was intended, and it's time to go home. Of course it is a privilege to be so popular, but sometimes it isn't quite the life it seems to be.

One of the things that I have witnessed many times is when prices were raised on items simply because it was George Jones, and he had money. It happened on houses, cars, and furniture. You name it, and it cost George more money than normal people would pay for the same items. I recall one time George was going to buy a TV. George wanted to buy things quickly and get out. That particular day, the salesman told him the price was $1,300.00 for the set. George didn't buy it, but he did tell me about the deal and the price. I was furious! I told George to give me a thousand dollars, and I'd get the TV and have it delivered. George didn't think I could get it that cheap, but he let me try. I took the $1,000.00 and went to the appliance shop. I told the salesman that I wanted to buy the TV and would give him $1,000.00 cash, tax included, and they'd have to deliver it. The TV was delivered that day to George's home. Why? The salesman didn't know I was buying it for George, or that I even knew him.

There's no telling how many rings, watches, gold pieces, chains, boots, leather jackets, cars, trucks, boats, guitars, and dollars George has been conned out of or given away. He was an easy-going man, but sometimes he allowed himself to get the short end of the stick in a deal just to find out about the person dealing with him, and then he would stay away from that person and never have any more to do with him or her. It was his day of reckoning.

I feel that Peanutt and I have been wronged, and that somebody somewhere is responsible for driving a wedge between George and us. I know that we never intended to hurt George in any way. Peanutt never took advantage of George, and they were very close, but the last few years we no longer had a social relationship with him.

Peanutt wrote seventy-one songs that George recorded and of that number, thirty-four were released as singles. The seventy-one songs included sixteen duets Peanutt wrote for George and Tammy Wynette.

Tammy recorded fifteen of Peanutt's songs. Peanutt was the sole writer on several of the songs, and others were co-written with George. Peanutt and Tammy co-wrote some of her songs, and he also co-wrote songs with me. The elite list of music Peanutt wrote or co-wrote saw several that hit No. 1 on the National charts, and some were BMI award winning records.

George and Peanutt always had fun when writing together. They could knock out a hit song in thirty minutes. Someone in Nashville became jealous of our relationship with George and Tammy. They started a bunch of rumors about George and me, and Tammy got upset and angry because someone told her a vicious lie. They tried to make her believe that George and I had an affair going on, but it was only another conspiracy to break up our friendship.

They succeeded.

Tammy would not allow George to come around us, but finally George realized what was happening, and he started coming to visit us, and he didn't care who didn't like it. He knew the truth, so he did what was right.

I understood why the entire mess happened. I loved Tammy and still cared for her after she and George divorced, but I knew exactly who fabricated and invented all the lies. They could not tolerate Peanutt going into the studio with George and Tammy to record six songs on one album, and they'd get one song cut that three people had co-written which meant they only got one-third each of the royalty stream of only one song on the entire album. This was more than they could take. They had to stop the camaraderie between George, Tammy, Peanutt, and me, and that would put a stop to the song writing and recording.

The only way they could succeed with their evil plot was to get between Tammy and me. They succeeded with their scheme, Tammy got totally sideways with me, and she broke her ties with Peanutt shortly after.

The bad people had gotten their way. They began to get more of their songs recorded and especially by Tammy. They successfully got rid of us, and they wasted no time moving in and taking over the territory and with Tammy gone, they only had George to maneuver and manipulate.

They kept George away from us, and it was difficult to know how they pulled it off, but there is one thing for sure, God knows everything about it, and the people responsible for misleading George and Tammy will one day pay on the Day of Reckoning. The Lord knows who's in the right, and who's in the wrong, and it will all come out one day.

Peanutt and I have survived, the wounds have mended, and we are very happy with our lives because we have forgiven everyone who harmed us. We have no complaints or any malice against anyone. The music industry can be so gratifying, but it can also be very cruel. We understand it; we've been in it all our lives, and we've been blessed more than we could ever imagine.

CHAPTER TWENTY

Reflections

George never owned anything for very long, and it is not difficult to understand why? His possessions were always at risk, and were either taken away from him by some failed transaction he found himself undertaking, a divorce settlement, or being cheated out of everything. People would convince him do all these big deals and if they turned out badly, George paid the consequences.

George never looked at deals in detail, and he trusted people too much. The thugs were good at making things look better than they actually were, and George was the one who took all the risks. Most of the ventures George got into, he never considered researching or finding a good solid business consultant to guide him. He just signed papers without reading them, and his business associates knew he wouldn't read twenty pages of fine print. George knew nothing about the deals except what they told him, and he trusted whoever was managing the business to handle all the detailed matters.

It seems George was always on the short end, while the others made all the money. Because George signed the contracts, he was left to fulfill them. Many times it was too late when he found out the deals were bad. He would rebel and refuse to honor his signed agreements and would wind up being sued for thousands and thousands of dollars.

I never could understand why anybody wanted to be a partner with George Jones. If he was such a drunk, a no show, an idiot, and a bad guy, then why did everybody want a piece of him? Think about it! He was a product you could market for money. They sold his famous name, but he never seemed to gain. The managers said George Jones was broke, but they were never broke! They made their living off of managing a broke man who never showed up for shows and was always drunk. If this is all true, then where did they get their money? Makes you wonder doesn't it?

George was up to his neck in IOU's and down to his last dime. He had to file for bankruptcy. How did he get in this kind of shape? It is always puzzling when big stars end up in bankruptcy court after they have made millions and millions of dollars. Most of these people are not good businessmen and women, and they waste money. This was not George's situation. He was manipulated and cheated out of his money and ended up owing the people who cheated him.

George was like a big company that went broke while all the people working got rich. That can happen if the employees are stealing seventy-five percent of the revenue.

Drinking was George's nemesis. When he would get on a drunken spree that lasted a week, he would end up owing somebody a lot of money. He ended up with the blame, shame, and bad name, but his co-workers never suffered; they got paid.

George needed help, but it wasn't the crooks who stole from him that came to help him; it was his dear friends in the music business that showed up. Johnny Cash, Waylon Jennings, Willie Nelson, and others that loved him came to his rescue. No one who got rich off George's career raised a finger to help him. His real friends who could relate to what was happening to him became a light in George's darkest hours.

George was too good for his own sake. He was 24-karat gold to the gold digger. It wasn't that George was ignorant, dumb, or naive. He had a philosophy that when he paid people to do a job, he shouldn't have to worry about it. The problem was he hired the wrong people. They drew out his gullible weaknesses and laughed at him all the way to the bank.

Part of the fun of being a star is having people at your beck and call. Everything is set up for you, and you shouldn't have to worry about anything except showing up and performing. George struggled with the people who worked for him. It seemed that every time somebody left him, he would owe the person a lot of money.

When George moved away from Florence, Alabama, he didn't owe Peanutt and I a dime, and we never tried to fabricate or find something we could bill him for just because he would pay it. Our friendship was free and along with that came a lot of free services. We didn't make him pay us for the little things we did. We were a lot like George. We trusted people and took them at their word. We never had a contract of any kind with George on songs we co-wrote with him, or any other business we did.

We knew who was getting paid and when it came time for everybody working on a project to get the credit they deserved, they all got it. Peanutt would have given more to George than he would ever have taken, and George knew that. You won't do wrong to someone if you love them for whom they are and not because they have money. That's the way George was. He felt everybody thought just like him, so he trusted people way too much.

Shug Baggot was aware of the harm cocaine was doing to George. He didn't care because George was a big user, and Shug was a seller. Why would Shug want George to stop? Who wants to lose a good customer like George? George was hitting the drug every day, and nobody cared. In fact, I believe they may have wanted him to die. Who knows what they were hoping for? Maybe a large life insurance policy, George's expensive jewelry, or a whole lot of other things they could gain from his death.

George's managers robbed him blind, but the worst thing that happened to George was that he was robbed of the fellowship of his dearest friends. Peanutt and I were not allowed to get near George, and that long close relationship we had with our dear friend just went away because of these evil concoctions that destroyed our friendship. We know George would have called us or come to visit us if he could have gotten away with it but for some unknown reason, he would suffer consequences if he tried to see us.

The so-called managers managed to get him into debt. He owed Tammy $36,000.00 in back child support. He thought his managers were taking care of Georgette. He owed a big bill at a furniture store that he thought had been paid. He was shocked when the IRS came after him for back taxes he thought had been paid. I know this personally because I was there when George told his managers to pay these bills.

George was an emotional wreck. He had been blindsided over and over. He made money, but the money was going for everything except the bills he owed, and the stress and burdens he was carrying made him just about give up on everybody and everything.

One of the happiest times of George's life was his marriage to Tammy Wynette. Even though I've spent a lot of time in this book talking about that marriage and the stories that followed, I know some of his fondest memories were during the time he was with Tammy.

I loved spending Christmas with George and Tammy at their house. George was as much fun as the kids. He enjoyed watching the girls rip open their presents, and he seemed to relish the moments as much as if he were receiving the gifts himself.

This was prime time for those children. Their parents were on the road a lot, so being home and gathering around the Christmas tree for some real family fun was as good as it could get for those children.

There was plenty of fun and plenty to eat. Tammy loved cooking, and she was very good at it. She would bake all sorts of cookies, candies, melts, cakes, pies, and banana pudding. She made her Christmas meals with good old country cooking. Her favorites were chicken and dumplings, ham, pinto bean, and cornbread. She had that country cooking knowledge of how to bring a meal together that would absolutely make you glad when you sat down at the table. Al Gallico, Tammy's business partner, was eating with us one Christmas, and he took a piece of her cornbread, wrapped it in tinfoil, put it in his suit coat pocket, and took it back to New York with him. That's how good she could cook. Al said he had eaten at the finest restaurants in the world, but he never found anything that was as tasty as Tammy's cornbread.

Tammy's cooking speaks for itself, and we talk about the good food she made to this day. She was not only a great cook, but she was a great wife and mother. I can testify to that fact because Peanutt and I were with George and Tammy almost every day of their married life.

Peanutt and I were very close to George before he and Tammy were married, and we remained close friends with George after they divorced. We would love to have remained friends with Tammy as well after the divorce, but the divorce caused so many divisions it was impossible.

Peanutt and I did not want George and Tammy to split up. We loved both of them, and we loved them as a couple. They loved each other, but just like every marriage, there were problems that needed to be worked out. They worked at it for several years until the walls of their marriage came tumbling down because the jealous songwriters started putting negative thoughts in Tammy's head about George. They knew what would upset Tammy and how to make her take action. Their efforts worked well to their own benefit. If you don't think so, look at what happened after they got Peanutt and I out of the way.

George Richey took over, and he could not make it obvious at the time, but he had his plan in mind a long time before the divorce. I want to set the record straight, right here, right now.

I never ever saw George Jones with another woman while he and Tammy Wynette were married, and I was with them every day. When George and Tammy were fighting, George would often leave the house and go get drunk. Most of the time when that happened, he was at our house. We'd play music, cut up, act like fools, tease each other, talk about the miserable businessmen they both knew, and George and Peanutt would drink.

Those jealous people who wanted to destroy our relationship created their own stories and told them to Tammy. They used their lies as a weapon and as tools to separate George and Tammy. They painted a picture in Tammy's mind that George and Peanutt were out womanizing and drinking and living it up. That's absolutely a lie.

In the first place, I hated alcohol and fought Peanutt tooth and nail about it. Our biggest troubles were over Peanutt's drinking habits. The reason Peanutt and I have stayed married for forty-five years is because we have hardly been apart. We love each other. I didn't care what the cost was, or what people thought of me. I was determined that Peanutt Montgomery was not going do things without me if he was going live with me. Peanutt knew I'd go to any amount of trouble to find out where he was, and what he was doing. He knew he'd better be where he was supposed to be (the few times he was somewhere without me), and he knew I'd check him out and make sure he was there. I got criticized a lot for the way I was, but I didn't care. I was looking out for the man I loved, and I would go to the ends of the earth to protect our marriage.

George knew me well enough to know it would be hell to pay if he tried to involve other women with Peanutt. That was the one thing that would have made me put a stop to their friendship. George and Peanutt were very seldom anywhere by themselves. I would never trust two men off together drinking with no one looking over them. George didn't care about me tagging along, and neither did Peanutt. It wouldn't have mattered if they did care; I would still have been with them. Peanutt came first in my life. I laid everything else aside and took charge of our marriage. I appreciated Peanutt's talents and respected his job of writing songs, but none of that gave him the right to do as he pleased. If he had not been a drinker, I would have trusted him more, but I'd seen too much.

It blew my mind when I found out George Richey and

Tammy Wynette were dating. George Richey was supposed to be George Jones's friend. While George and Tammy were married, George Richey and his wife Shelia were always around the offices with us, and they would come to George and Tammy's house, and we would eat dinner together. Shelia even babysat with True (our daughter) several times. She was a real sweet lady and absolutely idolized her husband. He was her life. Sheila's parents were deceased, and she had no other family except a brother who lived in Los Angeles, and she very seldom had contact with him. She was Al Gallico's Secretary. She dated George Richey for eight years before she married him, and it was the happiest day of her life.

Sheila was my friend and when we lived in Nashville she and George Richey came to our house often because George Richey wanted to write songs with Peanutt. They did co-write songs but only a few.

When all hell broke loose with George and Tammy, George Richey was sitting there ready to go. He had a master plan, and he was a con-artist who could make them work. Shelia was placed on the road with Tammy. Shelia helped Tammy in every way she could (unaware of what her real purpose of being with Tammy was).

Shelia helped with the girls, and she was Tammy's Matron of Honor at her wedding to Mike Tomlin. She was a loyal friend to Tammy. She turned against me when George and Tammy divorced. Shelia and I had been very close friends but to satisfy Tammy, she had to turn her back on me. Tammy had been told that George and I were having an affair, and that I was the one George wanted to be around instead of Peanutt. There were all kinds of lies told on me, but that was the master plan. George Jones would never have treated Peanutt Montgomery the way George Richey treated George Jones.

I would never have had an affair with George Jones. George was Peanutt's best friend, so how sorry a person would I have been if I had done that? George respected me as a person too much to come on to me. I'll admit that I loved George Jones. I loved him before he ever married Tammy. I loved him while they were married. I loved him after they divorced, and I loved him til the day he died, and I still love him. It's no secret that I've ever tried to hide. There is nothing wrong with loving somebody, and it's not because he is a legend or a country music star. I'd love him just as much if he were homeless.

I knew George Jones, and I loved and respected him as the person I knew he was. I could care less who likes it, and who doesn't. I'll always love and respect George but make sure you understand me. Love does not have to involve sex. I did not have a sexual type relationship with George. The good part of the whole thing is that I know the truth and better yet, George knew the truth, and anybody that would accuse us of such a relationship had to have some kind of ulterior motive.

George and Tammy divorced. The relationship between George, Tammy, Peanutt, and me was dissolved. George Richey married Tammy. George Richey's ex-wife, Shelia, died (mysteriously). Tammy Wynette Richey died (mysteriously). George Richey gained all of Tammy's career assets and achievements. George Richey married a young woman, who was Tammy's friend. They had a child and moved to Texas. George Richey died in Texas. The master plan worked exactly the way it was planned.

I feel so sorry for Tammy's girls. They were deprived of any of their mother's belongings and keepsakes. They received absolutely nothing from Tammy Wynette's estate. George Richey gave each of them five-thousand dollars. That's it! It is a shame for the girls to have that happen to them, but that's the way it is with a con-artist; nothing or no one gets in the way of what they want, including cheating the children out of what rightly belonged to them.

Tammy died. The entire estate was executed by George Richey, and there was seemingly no reprieve. He controlled and dispersed the inheritance only in the direction he wanted it to go. Tammy's girls were cheated out of what was rightfully theirs, and it is one of the worst situations of greed I have ever witnessed.

They never asked for much. All they wanted were little things like their mother's favorite necklace, scrapbook, photo album, or diary. What child wouldn't be granted those things? What kind of person would put more value than a child's memories on those things? "My God," I thought many times, how could anybody be so cold and greedy? It makes me sick, and Tammy would be clawing her way out of the grave if she knew how her girls were treated and cheated. It's absolutely sinful. My heart goes out to Gwen, Jackie, Tina, and Georgette.

I don't put anything past a person who loves prestige, money, and control over all else; especially, when his life is hampered by someone with severe health problems. The illness becomes a burden when there is some young, pretty, and healthy person waiting deceitfully on the side, so he can proceed with his plans when the person standing in the way is gone.

In Tammy's situation, a simple divorce would create too many losses for the perpetrator to absorb. In my mind, no doubt there was a plan that needed to materialize, and it all came about after Tammy died. The lights came on, so the world could see what really happened. I don't think there's a person alive who knew Tammy that is in the dark concerning how Tammy died, and what her life was like at the end.

George and Nancy Jones were right there to support the children Tammy left behind. They demonstrated true love and a heart for the well being of those kids. George helped raise those girls, and he knew all four of them were good girls. He loved them.

Life is a beautiful and wonderful thing but unfortunately, there are people who do awful and hurtful things, and there is seemingly no good moral or logical reason to their motives. If there is one thing I have learned from George Jones, it's the statement he made to me, "Don't ever hold a grudge." I do not hold any malice against anybody for the lies, the gossip, the rumors, the false accusations, and the misleading statements that were directed and made against Peanutt and me. I do forgive them, but I will never be associated with those people ever again. Just because Jesus said for us to forgive our enemies and those people who have hurt us, doesn't mean we have to kick around with them all day. I know who these people are even though many of them don't think I do, and I in no way will I ever again get involved with any of them in any form or fashion.

The part that floors me is that after their friendship with George Jones ended, these people who betrayed us tried to strike up a new relationship with Peanutt and me. They acted as if nothing ever happened, and they did no wrong. In my opinion, all they wanted was to exploit our connections and get themselves in the limelight for their own benefit. Sorry, but that will never happen. When we lost our friendship with George Jones through the deceit and lies of so-called friends, it was the end for us!

I want to make sure everybody reading this story understands that Peanutt and I loved Tammy Wynette. I am obviously still hurting because of the way our friendship ended, but I loved and respected her. Of course we loved George Jones, but we couldn't stop a large and powerful force that was intent on getting us out of the picture. The movement was so powerful that it broke up George and Tammy's marriage, and it destroyed our beautiful loving friendship.

The whole program was destroyed. Peanutt and Charlene were gone, Billy Sherrill was gone, and who was left? One man took control of everything, including the songwriting, the booking, the producing, and ended up with everything George and Tammy built. The ravaging of the Jones/Wynette children didn't end with Tammy.

The loss of George Jones has also been a very painful experience for all those who loved him, but the public doesn't know half of the story concerning the pain and suffering his children Jeffrey, Brian, and Georgette have endured over the loss of their daddy.

When it was discovered a few days before his death that George was expected to die, the children were never called, and they had to hear the news from relatives. They were never given the opportunity to come and stand by their daddy on his deathbed. George Jones's children were treated as total strangers when they came to the funeral. They were never recognized or their names mentioned. In fact as unbelievable as it may seem, their names did not appear in the Obituary.

The children stood in line at the Opry House for one-and half-hours with the rest of the fans who came to pay respects to George Jones. They were not given a V.I.P. pass as all the ones who sat in the important persons section were given. They entered the Opry House but as soon as they got seated, they were asked to move to another section to avoid being seen by the cameras.

The funeral was over, and you would expect that George's children would be escorted to a waiting limousine to be driven to the graveside memorial as Nancy and her children, family, and friends were. They were shunned extraordinaire and excluded from the traditional dinner that families have at the home of the de-ceased. They were not invited to their own daddy's home to reflect on his life with his family and friends.

Helen is George's only surviving sibling. She was ninety-one years old and made the trip all the way from her home in Texas to pay her last respects to her famous brother. Her name was never mentioned at the funeral; even though, Helen was George's favorite sister. In fact, George and Nancy were married in Helen's home, and yet she was unimportant enough to be left completely out of the ceremony of his death as if she never existed.

I sat about five rows back from Nancy. She was sitting on the front row near the casket next to former First Lady, Laura Bush. Nancy was surrounded by her family, friends, and her daughters, who are not George's biological offspring or adopted by him as Tammy's three daughters were.

Several country music artists took the stage and performed some beautiful songs to pay tribute to the Legend of George Jones. The minister gave a heart-warming message that consoled the grieving family. He spoke kindly and warmly of George. Below the stage sat a beautiful bronze coffin covered with an array of gorgeous white flowers and inside sleeping peacefully, lay George Jones, The King of Country Music.

George's four biological children, Susan, Jeffrey, Brian, and Georgette, his sister, many country music stars he mentored, and a world full of country music fans who idolized the Legend were in attendance that day. It was truly a celebration fit for a King.

When the funeral was over, I was overcome with the strangest feeling. I felt like I was watching a beautiful Rolls Royce rolling down a large avenue with no hubcaps and two flat tires.

As elegant and prestigious as this entire affair was, something was very much missing that denigrated the entire ceremony. The omission of George's own flesh and blood was substituted by people who had only known him a few years. The event was sad and painful.

Can you imagine a world where no music is playing, a church where no one is praying, or a sky that has no blue? That is the picture Nancy Jones drew and has shown to the world.

Sadly, the knife that was stuck in the backs of these children was twisted even deeper when it was announced that Nancy Jones inherited every single material possession George Jones had. The children were excluded from the entire Estate with no explanation as to why? They could not, nor cannot get so much as one of his beloved guitars, a pair of his famous boots, or even a sympathy card. Nancy Jones has them eternally blocked from anything of their daddy's they rightfully deserve, and she is trying to stop the royalty stream George left Brian and Jeffrey as part of the settlement when Shirley Corley Jones and he divorced. The boys have lived on that money since they were children. Nancy wants it all.

Can you picture Heaven with no angels singing, or a church with no bells ringing? Have you ever watched the heart of a child break in two? If you have, then you understand what Nancy Jones has done to these children.

I praised Nancy Jones for her care of George and sticking with him through his trials of life. She helped him overcome his bad habits, nursed him back to health, and got him back on his feet but at the same time, she belittled his children and destroyed his relationship with them, and that fact was glaringly exposed at George's funeral and since then.

What possible insidious reason could she have for doing these things to the kids? She recently interviewed in a magazine where she claimed George put her through hell. She then claimed that it was worth it.

I have driven the nail as deeply as I can, and the public will do the rest as they become keenly aware of what is happening to this family. As far as I have taken it, it won't ease the pain and suffering these children are enduring in the sordid distain this woman has for George's family.

On September 12, 2013, George would have had his 82nd birthday. A great celebration took place at his gravesite. Eighty-two balloons were released in his honor, but Jeffrey, Brian, and Georgette were nowhere to be found. They were not invited. So here is another unanswered question in the minds of millions of people. Why not?

In November of 2013, Nancy Jones threw a huge celebration as a last tribute to George Jones. Dozens of stars were invited and participated as tickets were sold for as much as one thousand dollars. None of the Jones children were there or extended the courtesy of an invitation. Again, why not?

The Country Music Awards held on November 6, 2013 was the grandest ever in its forty-seven year history. I was outraged that the Jones children were not invited. I am a member of the Association, so I called them.

"Why weren't the Jones children invited to the CMA Awards show?" I asked the person who handled my call.

I was told there were not tickets, but I insisted she put me in touch with somebody who had some authority.

"Oh, I can get them tickets, but they will have to pay for them," the smart lady claimed.

"How much will these kids have to pay for the tickets?" I asked the person in charge.

"Why, four hundred dollars," was her reply.

"They can't afford those tickets," I said.

Later that day, Nancy Jones Agent called me and chewed me out for calling CMA instead of him, but I let him have a mouth full of venom.

"Stop calling them kids!" He yelled. "They aren't little kids, they're grown adults!"

"Well sir, they're still the Jones children to me," I yelled back.

Would someone explain why I got that call shortly after I called CMA? Why does Nancy Jones hate those children as badly as she does? She turned on them with vicious poison as soon as George died.

George Jones was booked sometime in October of 2013 to perform his final and farewell concert. It is reported that when Nancy Jones questioned him as to why he was giving the producers the carte blanche, he reportedly said, "Because I won't be there." He wasn't. He died on April 26, 2013, and it was then booked as his final "no show."

The concert sold out for the November 22, 2013 concert tribute. The list of artists performing and attending reads like "Who's Who" in Country Music. Nancy Jones invited and reportedly paid the way for family and friends from Beaumont, Texas to be at the event but glaringly absent were the George Jones' natural children and his grandchildren.

My publisher was called the night of the concert. Georgette, Brian, Jeffrey, the daughters-in-law, or the grandchildren were invited or welcomed to the last tribute of their famous daddy. Sadness sets as the family feels the knife of bitterness and hatred sinks in. Nancy Jones says the family has started a scholarship fund for Middle Tennessee State University by the George Jones' family that she hopes will become a memorial to George. Which family? His real family, or his adopted family?

Sue Jones, wife of Jeffrey Jones said to my publisher, "It is a blessing in disguise. Georgette is performing near Houston, and we are going to unite for the first time in more than thirty years and enjoy Thanksgiving dinner together!"

The Jones children are not thugs or manipulative thieves. They are hard working men and women, who have jobs and struggle with life just like the rest of us. They aren't troublemakers who are always stirring the pot and making noise. Brian Jones is a Deacon in his church, and Jeffrey Jones is a dedicated Christian man raising his family with Godliness. They are quiet and good Christians, who will die of bleeding and broken hearts. It is time somebody fights back. My publisher, Dr. Sherman Smith, was incensed when he heard the stories of horror told to him by Sue Jones and sickened by the brokenness the entire family feels.

George always said, "There's gonna be a day of reckoning."

··

You Can't Judge a Book by its Cover,
A Hard Act to Follow and the Grand Tour

It would take a volume of books to contain all the stories a person could write about George Jones. Many of the tales about George paint a distorted picture of him. To be fair, there is some truth in many of the commentaries concerning his "colorful" character. His life had been rough in a lot of ways, but I am a defender of the fact that circumstances played a huge role in the choices he made.

According to the Scripture, a man has been blessed if he lives to the age of seventy-years old, and anything past that is an extra blessing. George Jones turned eighty-one on September 12, 2012. He enjoyed more than a decade of extra blessings. It's true that George drank a river of alcohol and sniffed sacks of cocaine. What made him do some of the things he did? It was definitely the alcohol and cocaine. Nine times out of ten, when George did something that was not good, he was messed up.

A person might ask why would George drink and snort cocaine if it made him do stupid things? George's addictions were a means of escape from a sometimes-painful world. I am not trying to justify his behavior, but he was not the man people thought he was. He was portrayed as mean and abusive when in reality, he had a heart of gold. Here is an example of George's kindness toward Peanutt and me.

Peanutt and I were sitting at our kitchen table drinking coffee one morning when George and Linda came over to visit. Peanutt had just finished building a model airplane, and he made mention that he wanted to fly it but needed a vehicle that could haul it to and from the fields where he would fly his planes. Nothing more was mentioned about this, and the subject was dropped.

The next morning, George called and wanted Peanutt and me to take him to the airport. On the way, George told Peanutt to turn and head toward the Datsun (now Nissan) dealership in Muscle Shoals.

When we pulled into the lot, George asked Peanutt how he liked the 280Z that was sitting there? Peanutt likes beautiful cars, so he enthusiastically said he loved it. George then asked Peanutt and me to check out the Datsun station wagon sitting nearby.

When Peanutt opened the door, taped to the steering wheel was a note on a yellow legal pad:

"TO PEANUTT AND CHARLENE,
Two of the greatest people I know. This is not for charity, this is a gift because we love you. You have written many a good song for me over the years, and maybe soon you'll write some more. I bought a car that I thought you could afford to operate, and a car you can afford. Hope we have many more good years together (as friends of course) HA!"
Love, George & Linda

(George had bought the 280Z for himself, and both cars were silver color).

George was grossly misunderstood. A man who is mean cannot be taken advantage of the way George was. His good heartedness ended up causing him pain. Inside that rough exterior was where a good person lived. You can't judge a book by its cover and believe me, I have read the book of George Jones and know the man inside and out.

George Jones was one of a kind, and there will never be another. Artists will come and go, but no one will ever replace George

Jones. When God made that mold, he threw it away. He's gone, so who is going to fill his shoes? The answer is nobody because it can't be done.

There have been many people who have tried their best to sing like George Jones. They've tried to imitate his unique phrasing, but no one has succeeded since he created his style back in the 1950's. He cannot be copied because there was something so special in his voice that allowed him to deliver a message in a song that would penetrate the deepest part of a person's heart. If I was a recording artist, I'd hate like the devil to have to follow that man on stage because once George finished singing, the show was over. He was the highlight of any performance. He grabbed the hearts of his audiences and when he was finished, no one felt they didn't get their money's worth. He was a hard act to follow.

George Jones started his amazing tour on September 12, 1931. His first feel of love was the embrace of his precious sweet mother's arms. He once said about his mom's cooking,

"After sniffing all the finest colognes and perfumes in the world, there's never been anything that could top the smell of mama cooking breakfast."

The first guitar that laid against his chest as his heart pounded with excitement demonstrated his love to sing and play for anyone who would listen and defined what he would do the rest of his life. The thrill of standing on the first stage he ever played at the Beaumont Playground in Texas embedded in him the need and desire to become the very best showman in the history of Country Music.

He wandered in and out of marriages like a needle weaving thread through a piece of fabric only to watch the seams unravel like the strings on a flower sack. The first marriage added a little piece of joy that he took on his journey; a beautiful daughter named Susan.

He had the honor of serving his country in the armed forces for three years. He fell in love the second time and became the husband of Shirley, and two more bundles of joy entered his life with the birth of his sons Jeffrey and Brian.

George's dream of a career in music and how it happened is a journey that's far more than fascinating. It's a phenomenon. He has soared like an eagle. He's flown the peaks of the highest mountains and to the lowest depths of the valleys. Tammy Wynette became the "First Lady of Country Music" when George married her, and he gained another gem of joy with the birth of his daughter, Georgette.

The dark days came and left a myriad of bad memories. The white substance (cocaine) added a heavy load to his life. George would love to have left this part of his tour behind, but the aftermath of that experience never left his mind.

George rode in his Rolls Royce like the streets were paved with pure gold, and then he'd find himself reeling from his horrific battle with drugs and alcohol that made him feel like he was riding on the meanest roller coaster at the world's largest fair.

George Jones grand tour ended on April 26, 2013, and those famous words "till death do us part" will live on in infamy. George came a long way through life and after many years of living, he found his resting place in the hills of Tennessee with his final and happy marriage to Nancy Jones and left behind the bad habits he picked up on his tour of life.

His life with Nancy reminds me of the songs *"Two Sparrows in a Hurricane"* recorded by Tanya Tucker and *"Islands in the Stream"* by Dolly Parton and Kenny Rogers. When George reached the end of his life's journey, I believe in his heart he was singing the words to his mother's favorite song, *"Nothing Between My Soul and My Savior."* A memory that has been from the beginning of his journey and will be there at the end.

Just before George died, the Pastor, who was the preacher of his funeral, was in the room with Nancy. The Pastor asked George if he was ready to meet Jesus?

"Well, yeah," he yelled, "Ain't you?"

A WORD FROM PEANUTT

On my first date with Charlene, we went for a ride on the Natchez Trace. We stopped at a picnic area for a walk. Charlene became occupied picking wildflowers, hunting for four-leaf clovers, and throwing rocks. At one point, I turned around to find her swinging on a tree limb. She appeared to be as free as a breeze and without a worry in the world. I knew right then that she was the woman for me.

I learned real quickly that when she didn't want to do something, all she'd say was, "Ain't no way." She meant exactly that, and the idea was nipped in the bud. On the flip side when she wants to do something, "It's gonna be done one way or another." I'm not surprised that she became inspired to write this book, and I had no doubt that she would write it.

I introduced her to George Jones in the early months of 1965, which was one year before we got married. George took a liking to her right off the bat. She literally hated drinking, and George was a drunk. I really didn't know how she would feel toward him, but she liked him. She's always told me that she looked beyond his faults and saw the good in him. It was a kind of sympathy.

George and I were always together along with Charlene. She stood by us through the days of our wild living. She was there to cheer us on when something good happened for us. She was there to lift us up in our lowest moments. She was a real source of encouragement for us to do better.

George and I were as close or closer than brothers. We were committed to each other. We had an unbreakable friendship, and Charlene became a great supporter of our loyalty to each other. When George and I had differences between us, she became the common denominator that would settle the problem. If we had a feud, she became our referee. She knew both of us as well as a mother knows her two sons. She spent many years of her life looking out for George and me. It wasn't unusual to find her in the kitchen at midnight cooking George something to eat in an effort to sober him up, or to find her packing a suitcase to go on a last minute trip to wherever George took a notion to go.

When Tammy and George got married, all four of us became very close. We spent seventy-five per cent of our time together. When they divorced, we stood by George. It was a very difficult time for him. When he and Linda Welborn (Charlene's sister) were married, we spent at least as much time together as we did with George and Tammy.

The hardest and most difficult times we had with George were the times spent between the marriages with Tammy and Linda. It was a short period of time, but the divorce was hard on him and everyone around him.

I once wrote a song entitled, *"What My Woman Can't Do, Can't Be Done."* George recorded it and released it as a single. I wrote that song about Charlene because it best describes her as she really is. She has been a lifesaver for me and a true friend to George. You will find this book to be amazing.

With my love to my wife,
Earl "Peanutt" Montgomery

The Legend of George Jones

TRACK 1 / DOWN TO THE RIVER
Vocals - Tosha Hill
Background Vocals - Leia Goodpaster
Gang Vocals - Leia Goodpaster, Reid Johnson & Kyle May
Acoustic/Electric Guitar/Resonator - Reid Johnson
Piano - Adam Mosley
Bass - Zach Witcher
Drums & Percussion - Kyle May
Claps - Reid Johnson & Kyle May

Edited and Mixed by H. Webster Tileston IV
Written by Earl Montgomery & Sue Richards

TRACK 2 / THE LEGEND OF GEORGE JONES
Vocals - Dinah Smith
Background Vocals - Reid Johnson
Acoustic/Electric Guitar/Banjo - Reid Johnson
Bass - Zach Witcher
Drums/Percussion/Piano - Kyle May

Edited and Mixed by Cory Wilhite
Written by Earl Montgomery & Paul Chisenhall

TRACK 3 / HIGH ON THE THOUGHT OF YOU
Vocals - Tosha Hill
Background Vocals - Reid Johnson
Bass - Zach Witcher
Drums/Percussion - Kyle May

Edited and Mixed by H. Webster Tileston IV
Written by Charlene Montgomery

TRACK 4 / HARD ACT TO FOLLOW
Vocals - Shelbie Z
Background Vocals - Leia Goodpaster
Electric Guitar - Reid Johnson
Organ Adam Mosley
Bass - Zach Witcher
Drums/Percussion - Kyle May

Edited and Mixed by Cory Wilhite
Written by Earl Montgomery & George Jones

TRACK 5 / WHERE THE GRASS WON'T GROW
Vocals - Tosha Hill
Background Vocals - Leia Goodpaster
Acoustic/Electric Guitar - Reid Johnson
Bass - Zach Witcher
Drums/Percussion - Kyle May

Edited and Mixed by H. Webster Tileston IV
Written by Earl Montgomery

TRACK 6 / SOMEDAY MY DAY WILL COME
Vocals - Tosha Hill
Acoustic Guitar - Reid Johnson
Piano - Kyle May
Upright Bass - Jake Johnson

Edited and Mixed by Cory Wilhite
Written by V.L. Haywood, Earl Montgomery & Christopher C. Ryder

TRACK 7 / A DRUNK CAN'T BE A MAN
Vocals - Tosha Hill
Acoustic/Electric Guitar - Reid Johnson
Piano - Adam Mosley
Bass - Zach Witcher
Drums - Kyle May

Edited and Mixed by Cory Wilhite
Written by Earl Montgomery & George Jones

TRACK 8 / ONE OF THESE DAYS
Vocals - Tosha Hill
Background Vocals - Reid Johnson
Acoustic/Electric Guitar - Reid Johnson
Bass - Zach Witcher
Drums - Kyle May

Edited and Mixed by Cory Wilhite
Written by Earl Montgomery

TRACK 9 / RIGHT WON'T TOUCH A HAND

Vocals - Tosha Hill
Backcground Vocals - Leia Goodpaster & Dinah Smith
Elecric Guitar - Reid Johnson
Organ - Adam Mosley
Bass - Zach Witcher
Drums - Kyle May

Edited and Mixed by H. Webster Tileston IV
Written by Earl Montgomery

TRACK 10 / WE'RE GONNA HOLD ON
(AIN'T LOVE BEEN GOOD)

Vocals - Tosha Hill
Background Vocals - Leia Goodpaster & Reid Johnson
Gang Vocals - Leia Goodpaster, Reid Johnson, Kyle May & Webster Tileston
Acoustic/Electric Guitar/Banjo/Resonator - Reid Johnson
Bass - Zach Witcher
Drums/Percussion - Kyle May
Stomps/Claps - Reid Johnson & Kyle May

We're Gonna Hold On Edited and Mixed by Cory Wilhite
Ain't Love Been Good Edited and Mixed by H. Webster Tileston IV
We're Gonna Hold On Written by Earl Montgomery & George Jones
Ain't Love Been Good Written by Earl Montgomery

TRACK 11 / KEROSENE

Vocals - Reid Johnson & Dinah Smith
Electric Guitar/Piano - Reid Johnson
Bass - Zach Witcher
Drums/Percussion/Sound FX - Kyle May

Edited and Mixed by H. Webster Tileston IV
Written by Reid Johnson

GENERAL CREDITS
Executive Producer - Paul Chisenhall
Producers - Reid Johnson, Kyle May & Zach Witcher of
Mint Music, Nashville, TN / mintmusicproductions.com.

GENERAL RECORDING INFO
All songs tracked at Oceanway Studios, Studio B, Nashville, TN,
with the exception of The Legend of George Jones - tracked at
Sound Emporium, Studio B, Nashville, TN.

All Overdubs tracked at Oceanway Studios, Studio C and
Jump Goat Media, Nashville, TN / soundemporium.com /
oceanwaystudios.com / jumpogoatmedia.com.

All songs tracked, edited, and mixed by H. Webster Tileston IV and
Cory Wilhite of Axis, Nashville, TN.

All songs mastered by Mike Monseur at Bias Studios, Springfield,
Virginia / biasstudios.com.